Featuring Prayers

PRAYERS that avail much®

to overcome ANXIETY & DEPRESSION

Germaine Copeland

Harrison House
Shippensburg, PA

Dedication

In honor of my uncle, Rev. Shelton Brock, a much loved and respected minister whose life and ministry lives on through his family. His ministry in word and music changed my life and the lives of many others. In spite of mood changes, he maintained a faith in God and continued to minister to congregations as a pastor and evangelist.

Acknowledgments

This book would not have been written except for the grace of God. I'm thankful for my teachers, the support groups, and facilitators who encouraged me in my pursuit to be the "me" God created me to be. I'm also thankful for those who attended my Bible study and prayer groups and the volunteers who worked side by side with me. I especially want to thank **Donna Walker**, who listened and helped me explore ideas about how to apply scriptural principles to feelings, emotions, and develop healthy relationships.

The people I owe the greatest debt to is my family. Since 1955, my husband, **Everette Copeland**, has loved and supported me and our family. He is a man of honor who loves God and laid down his life for me and our children and now for our grandchildren. He was always a diligent worker, who provided for us. In my darkest moments, even when he had no idea what to say to me, he provided the stability that our children and I needed. Today, he makes sure that I have the time and space I need for my continued writing schedule. Together, we seek to fulfill God's plan and purpose. Millions of people and I owe Everette Copeland a debt of gratitude. Thank you, Everette, for loving me through the good times and the bad times!

A special thank-you goes to **Ed Lauia**, a family and marriage counselor, who helped me focus on personal issues during a rough time in my life. I will ever be grateful for his valuable advice and support. He helped me collect my fragmented thoughts and uncover a painful past that I had forgotten but hadn't forgotten me. For most of my life, I had doubted myself and allowed others to write my story. Thank you, Ed, for challenging everything I believed. Some of my beliefs were solidified; others were changed. You helped me understand the dynamics of healthy relationships, and my life will never be the same.

I want to thank **Dr. John Turner, D.C.** who recognized the last attack of anxiety and depression and helped me avoid a breakdown. I will be forever grateful for his friendship and professional services. The trauma points I had been told to ignore were uncovered. I surrendered grievances against others and forgave! The physical pain left, and I felt like I had been born again, again!

Once again, the Harrison House team has blessed me with their professional and loving support. This book would not have been written without my editor and friend, **Kaye Mountz**, who has made this an altogether radical and life-changing book of prayers. Thank you **Brad** and **Kyle** and every team member who has been there to discuss the manuscript from beginning to end.

And we give **God** all the glory and honor and praise! Without Him, I would not be here, but with Him we have written the book.

"Since we have this confidence, we can also have great boldness before him, for if we ask anything agreeable to his will, he will hear us. And if we know that he hears us in whatever we ask, we also know that we have obtained the requests we ask of him."

1 John 5:14-15
The Passion Translation

Prayers and affirmations are paraphrased from the above-listed Bible versions unless otherwise stated.

Disclaimer: *Prayers That Avail Much to Overcome Anxiety and Depression* is written to encourage and edify readers with the Word of God and Christian principles to overcome all forms of anxiety and depression. It is in no way intended as a substitute for professional medical advice.

Published by Harrison House Publishers
Shippensburg, PA 17257

Cover design by Eileen Rockwell

ISBN 13 TP: 978-1-68031-707-7

ISBN 13 eBook: 978-1-68031-708-4

ISBN 13 HC: 978-1-68031-710-7

ISBN 13 LP: 978-1-68031-709-1

For Worldwide Distribution, Printed in the U.S.A.

2 3 4 5 6 7 8 / 25 24 23 22 21

Contents

3 – Anxiety

4 – Depression

5 – Hurt, Grief & Guilt

6 – Insomnia & Nightmares

7 – Panic Attacks & PTSD

8 – Suicide

9 – The Real You

10 – Germaine's Testimony

11 – A Message to Those Who Walk Beside Us

Foreword

By Timothy O. Goode, M.A.
Tampa, Florida

When I learned that Germaine was writing a book of prayers to overcome depression and anxiety, I was delighted. As a family and marital therapist for twenty-five years, I have watched many individuals struggle with these disorders. It is particularly relevant now. Fear and unforgiveness, which fuel depression and anxiety, are twin sleeves of the same straitjacket that holds many believers imprisoned, robbing them of God's provision and promises. Germaine speaks from personal experience with depression and anxiety.

As an earnest follower of Jesus Christ, she struggled for years with little help from the church or secular sources. The church has not always done an adequate job of helping people overcome depression and anxiety. Sometimes it is not enough just to believe and quote scriptures. Formulas don't always work. At times minimizing one's pain because of misunderstanding only deepens that pain and creates more isolation. I remember cringing in my pew one Sunday morning when a young preacher advised those who had been abused to "just get over it." There is no substitute for faith-filled expectant prayer and the continual renewal of the mind, which ultimately bring healing to the spirit, emotions, and soul [mind, body, and will].

While medical and psychological interventions may help, their relief is sometimes short-lived and inconsistent. In my experience, traditional talk therapy is greatly enhanced when it is performed as a joint prayerful exercise with a spiritual mentor or a trained and experienced Christian counselor [church take note]. I often felt as if the therapy sessions I conducted with my clients were holy times of prayer.

Along the same lines, the mood regulating neurotransmitters that are stimulated by prescribed psychotropic drugs can be divinely altered and permanently healed with prayers that avail much! Finding the right kind of medication along with proper dosing can be a laborious and discouraging process, sometimes with little or no results.

This is not a book to be read and laid aside. The prayers contained here have come at a precious price to the author. Each was carefully researched, thought through and prayed over. I know Germaine Copeland. I have heard her testimony and seen her life displayed. Each prayer is full of life and healing. They are not just rote recitations. Use them, pray them, meditate on them, and we will together thank our savior and healer, the Lord Jesus Christ, for the healing and deliverance they will bring.

Foreword

By Dr. Harvey Grahame-Smith,
MB, BS, MRCP (UK), MRCGP, DRCOG
Living Rivers Ministries
Ballymena, Northern Ireland

DURING my time as a general practitioner (family doctor) in the United Kingdom (UK), I saw the effects of both medical treatments and prayer both separately and together. I witnessed patients who were set free from schizophrenia, depression, suicidal thoughts, anxiety, grief, and fear as immediate answers to prayer. I also saw it happen gradually as a result of the combination of prayers and treatments. Also, families of people experiencing emotional and mental challenges were helped by prayers and by being able to pray.

The *Prayers That Avail Much* book series, by Germaine Copeland, has been used by God to change my life and that of others. To start with I just prayed the prayers. Later, I came to meditate on the verses and work the prayers and get revelation and make them my own. As I used them as a starting point, God has given me other scriptures to pray as well. Using these prayers, we know we are praying both God's Will and His Word. We know His Word has the power in it for fulfillment[1] and does not return void but accomplishes.[2] Once we get the Word in our hearts, it will come out of our mouths.[3]

1 Luke 1:37 AMPC

2 Isaiah 55:11 AMPC

3 Matthew 12:34 AMPC

This is a very timely book. Many are either experiencing the topics of this book personally or know someone who is. Jesus was (and is) anointed to heal the brokenhearted and to set the captives free.[4] This book is applicable to you if you are challenged by one of these conditions: if you are a family member or know someone who is affected, to prepare you for helping others or yourself, or if you will be ministering to others. As you make use of these prayers, let Holy Spirit set you and/or others free!

As you use these prayers, look to God as your source.[5] Let the divine and the health treatments work together to bring you the life Jesus came to give you—life in abundance, to the full, till it overflows![6] God's will is for us to be in health[7] and that includes all areas of our lives—spirit, soul (mind, will, and emotions), and body.

If you are experiencing one of these challenges in your life, you can always give these prayers to someone to pray God's Word over your life and see a difference. I learned this when I saw someone offer to pray for someone who was going through severe grief and depression after a bereavement. The person experiencing the grief, who was a faithful pray-er, was not able to pray in their usual way. The friend stood in the gap for them and prayed the Word over them, and the situation changed as they also did what the healthcare professionals told them to do.

These prayers are for each and every one of us to avail of! God is no respecter of persons. Prayer is communicating with Him, and these prayers will help you to pray effectively. The testimonies in the book will be an encouragement for, again, we know that God is no respecter of persons.[8]

---

4 Luke 4:18 AMPC

5 1 Corinthians 8:6 AMPC

6 John 10:10 AMPC

7 3 John 2 AMPC

8 Acts 10:34

A Letter from Germaine

Dear Friend,

There they sit just outside my window. I recoil as two huge, ugly black birds stare at me. I recognize them well and even know their names. Yes, Depression and Anxiety are back, but this time I'm grateful they are outside. I'm inside, hidden in the Secret Place of the Most High.

The book you hold in your hand is written from my personal experience with fear, depression, anxiety, guilt, and so much more. Even though God delivered me supernaturally, I soon learned that deliverance is maintained by faith. My deliverance was real! It was the beginning of a new adventure in faith.

And now begins your journey in faith! If you read and meditate and pray through the following pages, you also will experience transformation from the inside out. No one else can walk your journey but you. But you will never be alone because your heavenly Father will never leave you comfortless. He will never leave you without support.

Depression was a quagmire where I lived for many years. In those days, there wasn't a name for it; today it would be called "clinical depression." Anxiety was just a word to me until one afternoon when I felt my entire being fly into a million pieces, and I realized I was experiencing my first panic attack. Growing up in a minister's home, I had learned how to pick myself up, dust myself off, and put on my happy face! Today, I call myself a recovering people-pleaser!

Ultimately, there were days of emotional agony so great that I contemplated taking my own life. It is my prayer that as you read about my personal victory over mental disorders (page 216) and pray through the pages of this book, you will come to know God more intimately. I share about my tempestuous prayer experiences when I was learning to pray for our son who was in the lifestyle of addictions (page 121). Finally, to give hope to anyone who is thinking about suicide, I share about the day I had determined to end it all. But God!

These prayers were born from hardship that came to destroy me, and now I simply come along side you and share the powerful prayer therapy that increased my faith in the One who "understands humanity."[9]

Depression, anxiety, and other mental disorders are psychological strongholds to keep you blinded from the truth. You have the power to demolish every lie of the enemy "and break through every arrogant attitude that is raised up in defiance of the true knowledge of God."[10] God gave you the power of choice! You can turn depression, anxiety, and other mental disorders into blessings! "Nothing determines your choices, or how you react to the circumstances of life, except you."[11]

It is true—there are no quick fixes, but there is help!

This book is filled with help—scriptural prayers forged out of a desire to stay off the dark road leading to anxiety and depression. On my journey to wholeness, I discovered that when I prayed the Scriptures, God would turn on a floodlight for me, and I could see the path ahead.[12] My talks with God turned into the prayer therapy that continues to sustain me in my daily walk.

---

9 Hebrews 4:15 TPT

10 2 Corinthians 10:5 TPT

11 *The Perfect You,* Dr. Caroline Leaf, pg. 43

12 Psalm 18:28

Guiding You Through the Book

This book is written in **sections with topical headings** so you can quickly turn to the area of prayer you need. There you will find **powerful prayers** addressing both the problem and the solution.

When you first begin praying the following prayers, your feelings will not automatically change. Those old mindsets and familiar feelings will insist on hanging on! Nevertheless, I encourage you to **pray these prayers aloud** so you can hear your voice. These prayers will enhance any help you may be receiving from a health care provider.

From experience, I know that what we focus on will control our emotions and our behavior. When you focus on the prayers you most need at this time and pray them aloud, your spirit will absorb God's Word, which is being implanted within your nature, for the Word of Life has the power to continually deliver you. As you listen and respond to the scriptural prayers you are praying aloud, your mindsets that held you in dark places are being renewed to God's Word about you. The prayers become like poetry written and fulfilled by your life—yes, yours![13]

At the end of each section of prayers, you will find a short praise. This will give you something to hold onto! Remember, praise stops and silences the avenger.[14] **Keep these before your eyes by making these praises a vital part of your journey.** Copy them on Post-it notes or 3x5 cards and paste them around your house where you can see them. Mine were on my bathroom mirror, my refrigerator, my desk, and in my car. You can read them when you are stopped at a traffic light. Or record them on your phone and listen to them. This will help you keep God's Word before your eyes day and night.

Throughout the pages that follow, you will learn your **identity in Christ**, which will change how you believe, think, and feel about

13 James 1:21-22 TPT

14 Psalm 8

everything—including yourself. You will come to believe that you are here for such a time as this—at this moment in history. It is all by God's design, and He has need of you and the grace gifts He has deposited in you before the world began.

Included in this book are **testimonies** from others who have been set free from various levels of fear, harassing thoughts and worry, anxiety, depression, guilt, and more. Their testimonies will give you hope and inspire you! My friend, what God has done for others, He will do for you!

So, join me on this prayer adventure, and let us walk together on the road to a brighter day! You can begin now by praying aloud: "For the Lord God is brighter than the brilliance of a sunrise! Wrapping himself around me like a shield, he is so generous with his gifts of grace and glory. Those who walk along his paths with integrity will never lack one thing they need, for he provides it all!" (Psalm 84:11 TPT).

Your partner in prayer,
Germaine

First Things First

THE first step toward peace of mind and freedom from fear, anxiety, and depression—and every other mental and emotional challenge—is to walk hand in hand with the author of Peace and Love Himself.

I invite you to pray this prayer aloud with me now. Every prayer you pray hereafter in the pages that follow will build upon it and with faith and patience will bring you into a place of sweet peace and liberty, which is the abundant and blessed life God has planned for you.

A Prayer to Receive Jesus Christ as Lord and Savior

Heavenly Father, it is written in Your Word that if I confess with my mouth that Jesus is Lord and believe in my heart that You have raised Him from the dead, I shall be saved. Therefore, Father, I confess that Jesus is my Lord. I make Him Lord of my life right now. I believe in my heart that You raised Jesus from the dead. I renounce my past life with Satan and close the door to any of his devices.

I thank You for forgiving me of all my sin. Jesus is my Lord, and I am a new creation. Old things have passed away; now all things become new. In Jesus' name, amen.

SCRIPTURE REFERENCES

John 3:16 • John 14:6 • John 6:37 • Romans 10:9-10 • John 10:10
Romans 10:13 • Romans 3:23 • Ephesians 2:1-10
2 Corinthians 5:17,19, 21 • John 16:8-9 • John 1:12 • Romans 5:8

Fear

There is no fear in love; but perfect love casts out fear, because fear involves torment. But he who fears has not been made perfect in love.

1 John 4:18 NKJV

The Comfort of Your Luxurious Love

JESUS, even though I feel afraid, I choose to acknowledge that You are my LORD! You are my best friend and my Shepherd, and I shall not want for I always have more than enough. When I am weary, You make me to lie down in lush, green pastures, beside the still waters. You offer me a resting place in Your luxurious love.

When I feel overwhelmed, You restore my soul and lead me in the paths of righteousness for Your name's sake. Your tracks take me to an oasis of peace, the quiet brook of bliss. That's where You restore me and revive my life. You lead me along in Your footsteps of righteousness. Each step I take is leading me higher, even though it may seem I am going in circles.

Though I walk through the valley of the shadow of death, I will fear no evil. Your rod and staff comfort me. Lord, even when Your path takes me through the valley of deepest darkness, fear will never conquer me, for You already have! You remain close to me and lead me through it all the way. Your authority is my strength and peace. The comfort of Your love takes away my fear. I'll never be lonely, for You are near.

Thank You for preparing a table before me in the presence of my enemies—depression and anxiety. You become my delicious feast even when my enemies dare to fight. You anoint me with the fragrance of Your Holy Spirit, You give me all I can drink of You until my heart overflows. So why would I fear the future?

You anoint my head with oil, and my cup runs over with blessings, peace, and joy. Surely, goodness and mercy shall pursue me all the days of my life, and I will dwell in the house of the LORD forever. It's all in the name of Jesus!

SCRIPTURE REFERENCES

Psalm 23 NKJV, TPT

Love Banishes Fear

FATHER, You have not given me the spirit of fear but a spirit of power, love, and a sound mind. I do not have to fight against fear because, God, You are Love. Love's perfection drives the fear of punishment far from our hearts. Love banishes fear! I submit to You, and the temptation to fear terrorists, biochemical warfare, wars and rumors of war, and every other ungodly thing runs from me. I submit to You, the God who is Love, and proclaim that depression and anxiety are far from me.

Love has no fear because perfect love expels all fear. I live in God, and God lives in me. This way, love has the run of the house and becomes at home and mature in me, so I'm free from fear and all its evil companions of worry, anxiety, depression, and torment of any kind. There is no room in love for fear.

I refuse to impair my immune system through disobedience, and I resist the temptation to fear, which is a sin. Today, I let go of my continued striving and invite Yeshua into my heart and place my identity in the fact that He has already taken me into His heart.[15]

In Jesus' name, I will not give up. I will wait patiently because I am entwined as one with the Lord. This is the victory that overcomes the world, even my faith, amen.

SCRIPTURE REFERENCES

2 Timothy 1:7 • 1 John 4:8, 18 NKJV, MSG, TPT
Psalm 27:14 TPT • 1 John 5:4

15 *The Way of Love*, Ted Dekker, pg. 32

Safety Is Ours

FATHER, I lift up my family and myself and pray a hedge of protection around us. I refuse to fear for our safety in any circumstance because You, Father, are a wall of fire around about us to keep us safe. You have sent Your angels to encamp around about us.

In the name of Jesus, I choose to demolish every deceptive fantasy that opposes You, my God, and I break through every arrogant attitude that is raised up in defiance of the true knowledge of God. Lord, You will keep us forever safe, out of the reach of the wicked. Even though they strut and prowl, tolerating and celebrating what is worthless and vile, You will still lift up those who are Yours!

I ask that You end the evil tactics of the wicked! Reward and prosper us for You are the righteous God, the soul searcher, who looks deep into every heart to examine the thoughts and motives. I ask You, Father, to be our wraparound presence, our protection, and our defense. Thank You for bringing safety, comfort, triumph to us as we reach out for You. In the name of Jesus. Amen.

SCRIPTURE REFERENCES

Job 1:10 • Zechariah 2:5 • Psalm 34:7 • Psalm 91:14-16
Psalm 91:1-2 • Psalm 7:9-10 • 2 Corinthians 10:5 TPT • Psalm 12:7-8 TPT

Pleading the Blood of Jesus

DEAR Father, I plead the precious blood of Jesus over myself, my loved ones, and my property. I particularly plead the blood of Jesus over the portals of my mind and emotions. How privileged I am to apply this precious commodity that cleanses from sin, protects from evil, and seals the new covenant in my behalf.

In the Old Testament when the blood of the Passover lamb was applied to the doorposts of an Israelite's home, evil literally passed them over. This blood was symbolic of the blood of Jesus that would one day be spilled in our behalf as Jesus hung on the cross.

Now, under our new covenant of better promises, where I apply the blood the enemy also cannot trespass. On the cross, Jesus shed his blood for our sins and then made quite a trip from the cross to the throne. With His own blood, Jesus entered the Most Holy Place once for all time and secured our redemption forever! Before He seated Himself at the right hand of the Father, He poured His precious blood for me on the mercy seat of heaven.

Now, this blood gains me access into the holy of holies. It cleanses! It protects! And it draws a bloodline of safety wherever I apply it. Thank You, Jesus! In Your name, I pray, amen.

SCRIPTURE REFERENCES

Exodus 12:7,13 • Leviticus 17:11 • Hebrews 9:6-14 NLT • Hebrews 10:19
Hebrews 13:20 AMPC • Colossians 1:20 • Ephesians 1:7
Revelation 12:11 TPT

Snatched from the Brink of Disaster

TRAIN me, God, to walk straight so I may follow Your true path. Put me together, one heart and mind. Then, undivided, I'll worship You. From the bottom of my heart, I thank You, dear Lord. I've never kept secret what you're up to. You've always been great toward me—what love! You snatch me from the brink of disaster (fear and all its cohorts)!

Jehovah-God, the starting point for acquiring wisdom is to be consumed with awe as I worship. Wisdom will extend my life and make every year more fruitful than the one before. You are my Father, and I am Your child. I choose to listen to what You say and treasure Your commands. I tune my ears to wisdom and concentrate on understanding. I search for them as I would for silver, and I seek them like hidden treasures.

Then I will understand what it means to reverence You and gain knowledge of You. Thank You for granting me wisdom and a treasure of common sense. I choose to walk with integrity, and You are a shield to me. You have created faithfulness in my heart, and You guard my pathway. Thank You for giving me an understanding of what is right, just and fair, and showing me the right way to go. Wisdom has entered my heart and knowledge fills me with joy. Wise choices watch over me and understanding will keep me safe. Thank You for teaching me how to honor You. In Jesus' name, I pray, amen.

SCRIPTURE REFERENCES

Psalm 86:11-17 MSG • Psalm 86: 2:1-11 NLT

Lifted Up to Safety

FATHER-GOD, You strengthen my inner being by the promises of Your Word. I love Your clear-cut revelation. You're my place of quiet retreat; I wait for Your Word to renew me. Lift me up, and I will be safe. Empower me to live every moment in the light of Your ways.

Father-God, I waited patiently knowing You would come through for me. Then, at last, You bent down and listened to my cry. You stooped down to lift me out of danger from the desolate pit I was in, out of the muddy mess I had fallen into.

Now, I thank You for lifting me up into a firm, secure place. You steady me while I walk along Your ascending path. Every time I think about how You break through for me, I sing a new song. Ecstatic praise pours out of my mouth until everyone hears how God has set me free.

Many will see Your miracles. They will stand in awe of You and fall in love with You!

Father-God, I will not yield to fear, for You are always near. I choose to gaze upon You, for You are my faithful God. You infuse me with Your strength and help me in every situation. Thank You for holding me firmly with Your victorious right hand. You have shown me Your kindness and mercy when others oppose and oppress me all day long.

In the day that I am afraid, I lay all my fears before You and trust in You with all my heart. What harm can others bring to me? Father-God with You on my side, I will not be afraid of what comes. The roaring praises of God fill my heart, and I will always triumph as I trust Your promises. Jesus, You are my Lord. It's all in Your name, I pray, amen.

SCRIPTURE REFERENCES

Psalm 119:116 MSG, TPT • Psalm 40:3 TPT

Higher Ground

FATHER, in the name of Jesus, lift me up, and give me grace to trust You more. In these last days, I take my stand in the land of the living, and I will stand on holy ground. I will not be afraid because You will hide me in Your shelter in the day of trouble; You will conceal me under the cover of your tent. You will lift me high upon a rock, and my head shall be lifted up above my enemies.

I praise You with shouts of joy, singing, and making melody to You, my Lord and my God. "Lord, lift me up and let me stand, by faith on heaven's table land, a higher plane than I have found. Lord, plant my feet on higher ground."[16]

SCRIPTURE REFERENCES

Psalm 27

16 By Johnson Oatman: https://zionlyrics.com/higher-ground

Safe from Storms and Disasters

FATHER, we are grateful that not one word of Your Good promise has ever failed to come to pass (2 Kings 5:8). You are a loving Father who is good and faithful to Your children. My family and I are protected from every sort of evil in Jesus' name. We will not fear!

Earthquakes, famines, hurricanes, tornadoes, droughts, fires, tsunamis, floods, and more are the results of sin and its effects on a planet groaning and travailing under the "bondage of corruption" (Rom. 8:21-22). But You gave the earth to man and woman to govern (Ps. 115:16, Ps. 8:4-6, Gen. 1:26-28). Through Adam's disobedience, suffering and death were unleashed upon the human race. Natural disasters and weather patterns bring destruction to millions. But, Father, we know that You do not send them. Every gift from You is good and perfect!

We cannot control the events that transpire in this fallen world. We cannot declare there will be no more natural disasters or destructive weather. Your Word even predicts these events as we draw closer to the return of Jesus (Matt. 24:7a).

But we thank You that we can prevent natural disasters from coming to our homes and our properties. We can minimize their damage with our words. We can rebuke the wind and the waves and speak "peace be still" to storms just as Jesus did (Mark 4:37-41). We can speak just as Elijah did (James 5:17-18). And we can receive Your protection!

When floods roar like thunder and lift their pounding waves, we shout to You, our God. You are mightier than the violent raging of the seas, mightier than the breakers on the shore—You, Lord, are mightier than these!

You are a present help in time of trouble. You will never let me down, never walk off and leave me, so I boldly quote, "God is here, ready to help. I'm fearless no matter what. Who or what can get to me?" I pray this in the name of Jesus.

SCRIPTURE REFERENCES

1 Kings 8:56 • James 1:17 TPT • Romans 8:21-22 WEB
Psalm 93:3-4 NLT • Psalm 115:16 • Psalm 107:20 NKJV
Psalm 8:4-6 • Matthew 24:7 TPT • Genesis 1:26-28 • Mark 4:37-41
2 Corinthians 4:4 • James 5:17-18 • Hebrews 2:14 • Ephesians 2:6
Hebrews 13:5-6 MSG

Glorious Victory

FATHER-GOD, what marvelous love You have extended to me! You love me and call me Your child, and that is what I am! I stand in awe because I am loved by You, and I choose to let Your love continually pour from me to others because, God, You are Love. The light of Your love shined within me when You sent Your matchless Son into the world so that I might live through Him.

By living in God, love has been brought to its full expression in me so that I may fearlessly face the day of judgment and every other day. Why? Because as He is, so am I in this world.

This is love: You loved me long before I loved You. It was Your love, not mine. You proved it by sending Your Son to be the pleasing sacrificial offering to take away my sins. Such love has no fear because perfect love expels all fear. That means dread does not exist in my life, but full-grown (complete, perfect) love turns fear out of doors and expels every trace of terror!

With God on my side like this, how can I lose? If God didn't hesitate to put everything on the line for me, embracing my condition and exposing Himself to the worst by sending His own Son, is there anything else He wouldn't gladly and freely do for me? And who would dare tangle with God by messing with one of God's chosen? Who would dare even to point a finger? The One who died for me—who was raised to life for me!—is in the presence of God at this very moment sticking up for me. Do you think anyone is going to be able to drive a wedge between us and Christ's love for us? No way!

Nothing in the universe has the power to diminish His love toward me. Troubles, pressures, and problems—and all forms of fear, anxiety, and depression—are unable to come between me and heaven's love. None of this fazes me! Even in the midst of all these things, I triumph over them all, for God has made me to be more than a conqueror, and His love is my glorious victory over everything!

I'm absolutely convinced that nothing—nothing living or dead, angelic or demonic, today or tomorrow, high or low, thinkable or unthinkable—absolutely *nothing* can get between me and God's love because of the way that Jesus our Master has embraced me.

SCRIPTURE REFERENCES

1 John 3:1 MSG, NLT • 1 John 4:15-18 TPT, NLT, AMPC
Romans 8:31-39, TPT, MSG

My Bodyguards

Meditation

My friend! I encourage you to meditate on the imagery in these psalms and include your family in this prayer.

PRAYER

Father, sometimes it seems easier to depress than deal with personal issues, but I come before You today declaring that I sit enthroned under the shadow of Shaddai. You are the God of the Mountain, God the Destroyer of Enemies, God the Self-Sufficient One, God the Nurturer of Babies, and God the Almighty.[17]

I am hidden in Your strength, God Most High. You are the hope that holds me and the Stronghold to shelter me, the only God for me. You are my great confidence! I do not have to submit to anxiety attacks because You rescue me from every hidden trap of the enemy, and You will protect me from false accusation and any deadly curse or poisoned arrow.

Your massive arms are wrapped around me, protecting me. I can tun under Your covering of majesty and hide. Your arms of faithfulness are a shield keeping me from harm.

17 TPT Psalm 91:1 *Shaddai (šadday)* is taken from a Hebrew root word with many expressive meanings. It can mean "God of the Mountain, God the Destroyer of Enemies, God the Self-Sufficient One, God the Nurturer of Babies, God the Almighty."

I will never worry about an attack of demonic forces at night nor fear a spirit of darkness (fear, anxiety, and depression) coming against me. I resist the temptation to be afraid. Your protection and faithfulness are my bodyguards, for You are my hope, and I trust in You as my only protection. This I pray in the name of Jesus.

SCRIPTURE REFERENCES

Psalm 91:1-6 TPT • Psalm 25:21 TPT

Fear Vanished Without a Trace

My Father, who dwells in the heavenly realms, may the glory of Your name be the center on which my life turns. Manifest Your kingdom realm and cause Your every purpose to be fulfilled on earth and in my life, just as it is fulfilled in heaven.

I choose not to yield to fear, for You are always near.

I gaze upon You for You are my faithful God. Thank You for infusing me with Your strength and helping me in every situation. Thank You for holding me firmly with Your victorious right hand.

At one time, fear, anxiety, and depression raged against me, contending with me. But they have perished and disappeared. These demonic forces who warred against me have vanished without a trace!

I worship You, Yahweh, mighty God! You grip my right hand, and You have not let me go! I am no longer afraid because I know that You are here to help me! I hear Your whisper, "Be not afraid; I am here to help you." Thank You, my Lord and my God. I pray this in the name of Jesus.

SCRIPTURE REFERENCES

Matthew 6:9-10 TPT • Isaiah 41:10-13

Praise: Keep Calm and Carry on Praising God

Meditation

LET us offer through Jesus a continual sacrifice of praise to God, proclaiming our allegiance to His name.[18]

Praying prayers filled with the Word of God and praising God will help you stay focused on the God of breakthrough and freedom—your heavenly Father. Just as I chose to, you will learn to walk this journey by intentionally staying focused on your Creator who won your freedom for you.

Life is difficult![19] Jesus knew this![20] No one had ever told me this, and I thought life was against me—that I was a mistake going somewhere to fail, and it was God's fault. Be aware that the enemy of your soul wants to keep you trapped at a similar point. But your Savior is calling you to freedom and liberty. He wants you to know Him.

Some of us will go to quite extraordinary lengths to avoid our problems and the suffering they cause, proceeding far afield from all that is clearly good and sensible in order to try to find an easy way out, building the most elaborate fantasies in which to live, sometimes to the total exclusion of reality.[21] Praise takes far less mental energy. Praising the One who made you will energize and strengthen you for the day!

The prayers throughout this book are to help you align your thoughts with God-thoughts, and the praise will help you stay focused on God

18 Hebrews 13:15 NLT

19 *The Road Less Traveled,* M. Scott Peck, M.D., pg. 15

20 Matthew 7:13-14 TPT

21 *The Road Less Traveled,* M. Scott Peck, M.D., pg. 17

throughout the day. When those dark, anxious thoughts come, you must make a conscious decision to turn those thoughts into praise. Praise? Yes, because praise will stop and silence the avenger who is trying desperately to convince you to shut up. You replace those thoughts with praise, not because you feel like it, but because you are developing an intimate relationship with your Father.

Take a few deep breaths—stay calm and stay focused whether you feel like it or not. You will be moved by your feelings less and less. Dark thoughts will stop harassing you. Be patient with yourself.

You are not alone! The Holy Spirit is your Helper, and we who have walked this road before you are here to pray for you and cheer you on! God is on your side, and when you praise the One who made you, breakthrough happens! So, declare aloud, "Here we go," and turn the page.

Praise:

Bless the Lord, O my soul, and all that is within me bless Your holy name. I adore You and make known to You my adoration and love this day. I bless Your name, Elohim, the Creator of heaven and earth, who was in the beginning.

It is You who made me, and You have crowned me with glory and honor. You are the God of might and strength. Hallowed be Your name!

SCRIPTURE REFERENCES

Psalm 103:1 • Genesis 1:1-2 • Psalm 100

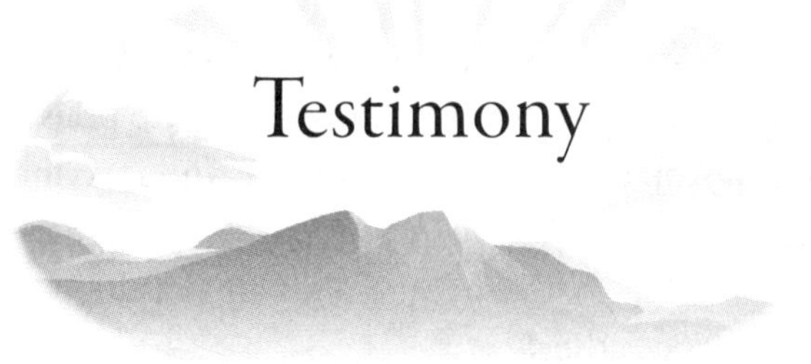

Testimony

Dare to Be Free

By Lynne Hammond

NOT long after I was saved, something horrible happened. Overnight, I went from being a happy, outgoing person to a doctor-described depressive. It was terrifying. Like cancer of the mind, darkness closed in and a mental battle began to creep into my soul. Thoughts of suicide hounded me day and night. Stomach ulcers wracked my body and turned it to what felt like skin and bones.

My spirit was saved, but my mind, will, and emotions were desperately ill.

A Spirit-filled psychologist told me he could give me medication that would help me cope with my condition. But only Jesus could make me free. I wanted to be free.

He pointed me to the path to complete freedom: Jesus. I didn't know much about spiritual things back then, but I did know one thing. The way to Jesus found me through reading the Word of God.

I literally meditated on the Word of God day and night.

Proverbs 4:22 tells us that God's words "are life to those who find them, healing and health [or medicine] to all their flesh" (AMPC). Just as someone takes medicine the doctor prescribes, I took the medicine of God's Word and applied it to my life.

You see, the Word of God isn't just nice-sounding phrases. The words you read are containers of the very substance of God Himself. As you read God's Word, the Holy Spirit imparts that substance to you—and God's power transmitted to you is what will change anything that needs to be changed in your life!

During the battle against depression, I meditated on the Word in a few different ways. When I would get up in the morning, I would read the Word — not large portions of it but just short sections. I would pick out one particular word in each passage of scripture that seemed to speak especially to my heart, and then cross reference it to other parts of the Bible. Then all day I would reflect on what I learned.

I'd also vividly imagine and even act out individual Bible stories. My favorite story was about the blind beggar, Bartimaeus, in Mark 10! I didn't just read that story; I lived it. I would picture myself sitting by the roadside, crying out to Jesus. I'd jump up and throw off that label of depression just like Bartimaeus stood up and threw off his cloak of blindness — and I would see myself free!

Another way I would meditate the Word was by taking a whole verse of scripture and carrying it with me all day long, turning it over and over in my mind.

I eventually began to see that the truths of God's Word could be applied directly to my life. I didn't need to simply read about the freedom I could find in God. I could actually live free! I may not have felt mighty, but because God was on my side, I was mighty! The more I meditated on truths such as this, the more they became a reality in my life—and that's when it was all over for the devil. Every time he sent a demon horde my way, I leapt to my feet, grabbed my Bible and acted just as God created me.

It wasn't long before the enemy quit coming. He eventually fled in total defeat!

Immersing myself in God's Word was a lot of work, but it was the most richly rewarding effort for me. After less than nine months of this kind of meditation, I was totally free.

Maybe you're fighting a battle similar to this. If so, I encourage you to get in the Word of God. Meditate it. Speak it. Pray it. Think on it. Act it out if necessary. Do whatever you need to get that Word rooted in your heart. Then rise up, take that sword of the Spirit and cut the devil to shreds with it. The Word is the truth, and the truth will make you free!

Lynne Hammond is a well-respected teacher and leader of prayer. She and her husband, Mac, pastor Living Word Christian Center in Brooklyn Park, Minnesota.

Harassing Thoughts & Worry

Pour out all your ***worries*** *and stress upon him and leave them there, for he always tenderly cares for you.*

1 Peter 5:7 TPT

Taking Thoughts Prisoner

DEAR Father-God, I choose to give myself to You because of all You have done for me. Let me be a living and holy sacrifice—the kind You find acceptable. This is truly the way I worship You. As I set aside the behavior and customs of this world, Your Word transforms me into a new person by changing the way I think. It will change me from the inside out!

I am learning to know Your will for me, which is good and pleasing and perfect. Thank You for delivering me from the spirit of depression and all the agony that comes with it. You have given me a spirit of love, power, and a well-balanced mind.

"I have learned that my thought life has incredible power over my intellectual, emotional, cognitive, and physical well-being. My thoughts can either limit me to what I believe I can do or free me to develop abilities well beyond my expectations or the expectation of others.[22]"

Therefore, although I live in the natural realm, I don't wage a military campaign employing human weapons, using manipulation to achieve my aims. Instead, my spiritual weapons are energized with divine power to effectively dismantle the defenses behind which I have hidden. With the help of the Holy Spirit, I can demolish every deceptive fantasy that opposes God and break through every arrogant attitude that is raised up in defiance of the true knowledge of God.

Today, I choose to capture, like prisoners of war, every thought and insist that it bow in obedience to the Anointed One. Since I am armed with such dynamic weaponry, I stand ready to punish any trace of rebellion—negative and tormenting thoughts, worry, anxiety—and bring them into obedience to Your Word.

22 *Think, Learn Succeed,* Dr. Caroline Leaf, pg. 34

With my soul I will bless the Lord with every thought and purpose in life. My mind will not wander out of the presence of God. My life shall glorify the Father—spirit, soul, and body. I take no account of the evil done to me. I pay no attention to a suffered wrong. It holds no place in my thought life. I am ever ready to believe the best of every person. I gird up the loins of my mind, and I set my mind and keep it set on what is above— the higher things— not on the things that are on the earth.

Whatever is true, whatever is worthy of reverence and is honorable and seemly, whatever is just, whatever is pure, whatever is lovely and lovable, whatever is kind and winsome and gracious, if there is any virtue and excellence, if there is anything worthy of praise, I will think on and weigh and take account of these things—I will fix my mind on them.

I have the mind of Christ, the Messiah, and do hold the thoughts, feelings, and purposes of His heart. In the name of Jesus, I will practice what I have learned and received and heard and seen in Christ and model my way of living on it, and the God of peace—of untroubled, undisturbed well-being—will be with me, amen.

SCRIPTURE REFERENCES

Romans 12:1-2 NLT, MSG • 2 Corinthians 10:3-5 • Colossians 3:2
Psalm 103:1 • Philippians 4:8 • 1 Corinthians 6:20 • 1 Corinthians 2:16
1 Corinthians 13:5, 7 • Philippians 4:9 • 1 Peter 1:13

Peace Is My Life Motto

FATHER, I turn my back on worry, and I do something good. I embrace peace and refuse to let it get away. I make peace my life motto! I crave peace and choose peace in my life. I go after it, and I work to maintain it.

When my life pleases you, Lord, You make even my enemies to be at peace with me.

Lord, You said, "I leave the gift of peace with you—My peace. Not the kind of fragile peace given by the world, but My perfect peace...." I will not let my heart be troubled and afraid. I refuse to be agitated and disturbed. I will do as Your Word says and cast all my care on You because You care for me (1 Peter 5:7). That means You care for and about me and love me, but it also means that You will do the caring—or thinking—for me!

So instead of worrying, I will pray. Father, I will let petitions and praises shape my worries into prayers, letting You know my concerns and thanking You for the answers. Your peace will keep my thoughts and heart quiet and at rest as I trust in Christ Jesus, my Lord. It is wonderful what happens when Jesus displaces worry at the center of my life.

Thank You for guarding me and keeping me in perfect and constant peace. My mind—both its inclination and its character—is stayed on You. I commit myself to You, lean on You, and hope confidently in You.

I let the peace, the soul harmony that comes from Christ, rule and act as umpire continually in my heart, deciding and settling with finality all questions that arise in my mind. I am thankful! I am appreciative! I am so grateful! I give praise to You always in Jesus' name, amen.

SCRIPTURE REFERENCES

Philippians 4:6-7 MSG • Colossians 3:15 AMPC • Proverbs 16:7 NLT
Psalm 34:14 MSG, TPT, AMPC, NLT • John 14:27 NLT, TPT, AMPC
Isaiah 26:3 AMPC • 1 Peter 5:7 NKJV

Exchanging Lies for Truth

Meditation

God gave you and me a free will. We can choose life or death. We can choose to eat from the tree of knowledge of good and evil—or partake of the tree of Life. We can choose faith, hope, and love, or we can choose negative thinking, worry, anxiety, and depression. We cannot blame others for where we are today. For all practical purposes, we choose to separate the lies from the truth. God's plans for you are for good and not evil. His plan for you does not include misery, depression, and gloom.

Although the multitalented woman Donnis Brock Griffin was told all her life that she could not learn math, she became a seamstress and a tailor where math is crucial. In her seventies, she discovered that what she had been told was not true! She had been doing what she had been told she could not do from the time she learned to sew that first garment.

It *is* possible to renew the mind to the Word of God. You can replace your statements of "I cannot" with "I can, and I will." You can replace thoughts of worry, fear, self-pity, and other self-defeating thoughts with peace. You can keep your mind filled with self-doubt, self-rejection, and become self-absorbed—or you can change your self-image by replacing the lies (more politely called negative thoughts and worry) with God's thoughts toward you.

Choose to learn and believe that you are the person God has created you to be!

"Regardless of what anyone has told you, you can learn. You can succeed at life. When you learn how to learn, exploring, understanding, and mastering the art of mental self-care, you can go beyond mindfulness, developing a whole mind lifestyle that allows you to transform your neighborhood, your community, your nation, and your world."[23]

Prayer

Heavenly Father, I bind my mind to the mind of Christ, my will to the will of God, and my emotions to the control of the Holy Spirit. I choose to walk according to the Spirit of Life in Christ Jesus, setting my mind on the things of the Spirit. To be spiritually minded is life and peace.

Since I have been raised to new life with Christ, I choose to set my sights on the realities of heaven, where Christ sits in the place of honor at Your right hand. Today, I choose to think about the things of heaven, not the things of earth. For I died to this life, and my real life is hidden with Christ in God.

I count myself dead to sin but alive to God in Christ Jesus. I know that Your plans for me are for good and not for disaster, to give me a future and a hope. When I pray, You will listen and when I look for You wholeheartedly, I will find You. Lord, I exchange lies for Your truth.

Jesus, You have set me free—not partially, but completely and wonderfully free! I choose to cherish this truth and stubbornly refuse to go back into the bondage of depression and anxiety. In Jesus' name, amen.

SCRIPTURE REFERENCES

Matthew 18:18 NKJV • Romans 8:6 • Colossians 3:1-3 NLT
Jeremiah 29:11-13

23 *Think, Learn, Succeed,* Dr. Caroline Leaf, pg. 34

Trusting God for Finances

Dear Father, I am Your child, and I need Your help. Financial concerns overwhelm me. But when I am afraid or overcome with thoughts, I choose to trust You rather than worry. Though I'm tempted to feel anxious and out of control, I choose to submit to You. I bind my mind, my will, and my emotions to the will of God. I bind my mind to the truth and to the blood of Jesus. I refuse worry, anxiety, and fear. Father, I choose to turn my anxieties into prayers and make my requests known to You.

If You give such attention to the appearance of wildflowers—most of which are never even seen—I know You will attend to me, take pride in me, do Your best for me. I will relax and not be so preoccupied with *getting,* so I can respond to Your *giving*. People who don't know You and the way You work fuss over these things, but I know You and how You work. I choose to steep my life in God-reality, God-initiative, God-provisions.

I forsake worries! Above all, I chase after the realm of Your kingdom and the righteousness that proceeds from You. Then all these less important things will be given to me abundantly. As I seek You above all else, You will give me everything I need.

Jehovah-Jireh, You are the One who sees my family's needs and provides for them, and we honor Your name. May the glory of Your name be the center on which our lives turn. Manifest Your kingdom realm and cause Your every purpose to be fulfilled on earth just as it is fulfilled in heaven. We acknowledge You as our Provider of all we need each day. Father, You receive all the glory and the honor throughout the eternity of eternities! Amen!

SCRIPTURE REFERENCES

Psalm 56:3 • Matthew 16:19 • Philippians 4:6 • Matthew 6:9-13 TPT
Matthew 6:25-33 MSG, TPT, NLT • Philippians 4:19-20 TPT

Aligning My Thoughts With God's Word

FATHER-GOD, I choose to exchange my negative thoughts for Your thoughts and align my thinking with Yours. I exchange my old negative mindset for Your thoughts toward me. I ask You, the God of peace and harmony, to set me apart and make me completely holy. And I pray that my entire being—spirit, soul, and body—will be kept completely flawless in the appearing of my Lord and Savior, Jesus. You called me by my name. You are trustworthy and will thoroughly complete Your work in me.

Father, before You shaped me in the womb, You knew all about me. You know everything there is to know about me spirit, soul, and body. You perceive every movement of my heart and soul, and you understand my every thought that has been the source of depression and anxiety. I am an open book to You. You know words that I will speak even before I start a sentence. Your understanding of me brings me wonder and strength.

Today, I choose to align my thoughts with Truth. You chose me to be Your very own, joined me to Yourself even before You laid the foundation of the universe. Because of Your great love, You ordained me so that I would be seen as holy in Your eyes with an unstained innocence.

Father-God, I choose to believe Your Word. As I learn to align my thoughts with Yours, You will give me wisdom and understanding about how to live victoriously in a world of polarity—darkness and light. I will no longer let my heart be troubled, distressed, or agitated. Instead, I believe in, adhere to, trust in, and rely on You.

Thank You, Holy Spirit, for being my Counselor, Helper, Intercessor, Advocate, Strengthener, and Standby as I walk out my deliverance from anxiety, depression, and worry in every form. You are the Spirit of Truth who will remain with me forever. Amen

SCRIPTURE REFERENCES

I Thessalonians 5:23-24 TPT • Jeremiah 1:5 • Psalm 139:1-6 TPT
Ephesians 1:4 TPT • John 14:1,16 TPT, AMPC

Surrendering My Cares to the Lord

FATHER, thank You that I have been delivered from the power of darkness and translated into the Kingdom of Your dear Son. I commit to live free from worry in the name of Jesus, for the law of the Spirit of life in Christ Jesus has made me free from the law of sin and death.

I align my thoughts with Your will and choose to bow low in Your awesome presence. In due season, You will exalt me. I'm here to pour out all my worries and stress upon You and leave them with You, for You always tenderly care for me. I choose to be well-balanced and always alert, because my enemy, the devil, roams around incessantly, like a roaring lion looking for its prey to devour. Today, I take a decisive stand against him and resist his every attack of fear, depression, and tormenting thoughts with strong, vigorous faith.

I cast the whole of my cares—all my anxieties, all my worries, all my concerns—once and for all on You. You care for me affectionately and care about me watchfully. You sustain me. You will never allow the consistently righteous to be moved—made to slip, fall, or fail! Father, I delight myself in You, and You perfect that which concerns me.

I cast down imaginations, reasonings, and every high thing that exalts itself against the knowledge of You, and I bring into captivity every thought to the obedience of Christ. I lay aside every weight and the sin of worry, which so easily tries to ensnare me. I run with patience the race that is set before me, looking unto Jesus, the Author and Finisher of my faith. I start running—and never quit! When I find myself flagging in my faith, I keep my eyes on Jesus and study how He did it. That shoots adrenaline into my soul!

Thank You, Father, that You are able to keep that which I have committed unto You. I think on (fix my mind on) those things that are true and honest, authentic and real, honorable and admirable, beautiful and respectful, pure and holy, merciful and kind. Summing it all up, I will fill my mind with the best, not the worst; the beautiful, not the ugly. I fasten my thoughts on every glorious work of God, praising You always.

I will not let my heart be troubled. I abide in Your Word, and Your Word abides in me. Therefore, Father, I do not forget what manner of person I am. I look into the perfect law of liberty and continue therein, being not a forgetful hearer, but a doer of the Word and, thus, blessed in my doing!

Thank You, Father. I am carefree. I walk in that peace that passes all understanding. In Jesus' name, amen.

Scripture References:

Colossians 1:13 • Hebrews 12:1-3 MSG, • Romans 8:2 • 2 Timothy 1:12
1 Peter 5:6-7 AMPC • Philippians 4:8 TPT, MSG • Psalm 55:22 AMPC
John 14:1 • Psalm 138:8 • James 1:22-25 • 2 Corinthians 10:5
Philippians 4:6

Praying (Not Worrying) for My Children

Meditation

SOMETHING just wasn't right! I remembered having that feeling when nothing was going on, but this time was different. I was seeing changes in my teenage son, but no one else, including my husband, seemed to notice. Somehow, I just knew, but I didn't know the questions to ask. No one would listen because I couldn't give them the facts they needed. In fact, I was accused of being suspicious, worrying when nothing was amiss.

Yet, I knew that something had changed in the behavior of my son, David, especially his eating habits. Suddenly, my teenage boy couldn't eat enough like many teenage boys, and sometimes he drank large quantities of milk. Yet, the next night he wasn't hungry at all. These were not his usual eating habits. Then the bombshell exploded! The unbelievable happened—he was addicted to drugs! We talked with teachers, counselors, psychologists, and psychiatrists only to discover there was no human solution to this problem.

It was more vital than ever before to know how to pray prayers that avail much. Each day with my Bible, pen, and notebook, I read, cried, talked with the Holy Spirit, and made notes. I read books on prayer, devouring the contents, and tried all the formulas with vigor! There in the inner chamber of prayer, I wrote letters to the Father, confident that the Holy Spirit was directing my thoughts and writings. I carefully penned meaningful scriptures, inserting David's name and those of other loved ones. As I reread the flowing words aloud before the Throne of Grace, my faith rose to new levels. God heard the cries of a desperate mother, and today, my son, David, is a transformed man now serving as Vice President of Prayers That Avail Much Ministries.

You see, my friend, I have not just written prayers to fill books of the PTAM series. I have lived these prayers. They were born from hardship that came to destroy my family, but instead, I trusted the Greater One and trusted His Word. And as I clung to His promises in fellowship with Him, God brought David and me through to victory. I simply share with You all that His Word has given me. What the devil sends to destroy you, God can turn into a triumph so big it will bless and help others far and wide.

David's complete testimony, "Set Free from 28 Years of Depression and Addictions" is found on page 117. My detailed testimony of how I prayed for him follows it on page 121.

Prayer

Father-God, I come before You today pleading for the deliverance and salvation of my children. You are my LORD, and my heart rejoices in You. My strength rises in You! My words mock my enemies because I rejoice in Your deliverance. No one is holy like You, the Lord—no, no one except You! I proclaim that there is no rock like my God! You are the LORD who knows, and You weigh every act.

I see through the eyes of my heart. I see my children walking with You all the days of their lives. Even before You made the world, You loved us and chose us. You chose my children—chose them to be holy and without fault in Your eyes. You are rich in kindness and grace, and You have holy plans for my children. You have a hope and a future for them. You have a prearranged plan for them to walk in the good life.

So I thank You that You give my children the spiritual wisdom and insight that they might grow in the knowledge of You. I pray their hearts will be flooded with light so they can understand their rich and glorious spiritual inheritance. I also pray that they will understand the incredible greatness of Your power for us who believe. Praise God, this is the same mighty power that raised Jesus Christ from the dead.

Thank You, Father, for laborers sent across the paths of my children—laborers to whom they will listen and who can lead them into the light of God's Word. In the name of Jesus Christ, there is nowhere they can go to avoid Your Spirit. If they climb to the sky, You're there! If they go underground, You're there! If they fly on morning's wings to the far western horizon, You will find them—You're already there waiting! Father, in the name of Jesus, I proclaim that all my children will be disciples taught by the LORD. They will be obedient to Your will, and great shall be their peace and undisturbed composure. My children were born to worship and glorify You!

SCRIPTURE REFERENCES

1 Samuel 2:1-3 • Matthew 18:18 • Psalm 139 • Isaiah 54:13
Ephesians 1:3, 7, 9-11, 17-19 NLT • Ephesians 2:10 AMPC
Jeremiah 29:11 • Jeremiah 1:5 MSG

On the Right Track

TODAY, with the help of the Holy Spirit, I demolish every deceptive fantasy that opposes God, and I break through every arrogant attitude raised up that is in defiance of the true knowledge of God. I capture, like prisoners of war, every thought and insist that it bow in obedience to the Anointed One. I'm not saying that I have this all together, that I have it made. But I am well on my way, reaching out for Jesus Christ, who has so wondrously reached out for me.

I've got my eye on the goal, where God is beckoning me onward—to Jesus. I'm off and running, and I'm not turning back. So, I choose to stay focused on that goal. I want everything You have for me. I totally commit to You, and You will clear my blurred vision. I'll see it yet! Now that I am on the right track, I choose to stay on the right track!

I will not be afraid. My redemption is nearer than when I believed. It's all in the name of Jesus.

SCRIPTURE REFERENCES

2 Corinthians 10:5 TPT • Philippians 3:13-16 MSG • Romans 13:11

Customize Your Thinking

FATHER-GOD, I choose to learn, understand, and use my mind for success and not failure. I am no longer controlled by mental anguish—depression and anxiety. You created me spirit, soul, and body, and I purpose to renew my mind. I am "always thinking and learning, every moment of every day."[24]

Your truth is a shining light guiding me in my choices and decisions—the revelation of Your Word makes my pathway clear and helps me choose how I think and feel. I am enfolded into Christ, and I am an entirely new creation. All that is related to the old order has vanished, and everything is fresh and new. When my mind is under attack, I choose to customize my thinking. I will not allow even a little lie into my heart that can permeate my entire belief system.

Thank You for Your compassionate mercy and for lavishing Your forgiveness on me. My thoughts are not like Your thoughts, and my ways are different from Yours. But today, I choose to obey You by aligning my thoughts with Yours. Not my will, but Yours be done in my life. I no longer need to be worried. Instead, I will pray throughout each day, offering You my faith-filled requests with thanksgiving.

I choose to tell You every detail of my life, and Your wonderful peace that transcends human understanding will make the answers known to me through Jesus Christ. I take responsibility for my thought-life and fix my thoughts on all that is authentic and real, honorable, and admirable, beautiful and respectful, pure and holy, merciful and kind. I choose to fasten my thoughts on Your glorious works, praising You, and You will be with me in all things. In Jesus' mighty name I pray, amen.

SCRIPTURE REFERENCES

Romans 12:2 • Psalm 119:105 TPT • 2 Corinthians 5:17 TPT
Galatians 5:9 TPT • Isaiah 55:7-12 • Philippians 4:6-9 TPT

24 *Think, Learn, Succeed,* Dr. Caroline Leaf, pg. 60

Don't Believe the Lies

Meditation

No matter what others may think about you, it is what you believe about yourself that determines how you react to the circumstances of life. It may have been in early childhood, teenage years, or even later when you believed a lie that opened the door for depression and anxiety to enter your life. Here is the simple truth: Wherever you find depression, you will find a lie that was believed. There is a lie at the bottom of it all.

We are born into a world of darkness to parents, who like all of us, make mistakes. In my own experience, my parents loved me and my siblings. My dad was a beloved pastor and Bible teacher, and my mother was a multi-talented woman who was subservient to her husband. We were to be examples to the other children in our church, which led me to believe that appearances were more important than relationships. I received the approval of adults when I looked the part of the "perfect" pastor's daughter, and as a result, I focused more on looking right than I did on loving others.

As you consider the following list of lies many have believed, let me encourage you to make your personal list and replace each lie with truth. Look for lies that destroyed your peace of mind, and answer them with God's Word. Once you identify the lie, you open the door to truth that will free you![25]

25 John 8:32 MSG

Exposing Lies:

- I am not good enough.
- I am not smart enough.
- I am stupid.
- I am a mistake.
- I am unworthy of being loved.
- I am a failure.
- I can never measure up.
- No one likes me.
- I can't do anything right.
- I'm not worth the salt in my bread.
- God is angry with me.

"You may feel you don't have any power over your life or circumstances, but you do! Your ability to think, feel, and choose is innately powerful and resilient—you have a mind that is more potent than all the smartphones on the planet combined! You can move from survival to success—and it all begins in your mind. In recognizing both the impact of your sociocultural context and your own thoughts, you can redefine your past, reimagine your present, and realize your future."[26]

Prayer

My God, a dark mood is attempting to move in on me, but I choose to lift up my soul into Your presence. You are here for me! You will not allow depression, guilt, shame, and anxiety to gloat over me or overtake me. Lord, direct me throughout my journey, so I can experience Your plans for my life. Reveal the life-paths that are pleasing to You, and escort me along the way. Take me by the hand

26 *Think, Learn, Succeed,* Dr. Caroline Leaf, pg. 30

and teach me. I pray that hidden things are exposed and reproved by the light. I walk flooded with light. Thank You for Your truth that makes me free!

For You are the God of my salvation, and I have wrapped my heart into Yours. Thank You for forgiving my failures. Give me grace, Lord! Always look at me through Your eyes of love—Your forgiving eyes of mercy and compassion. I have discovered how easy You are to please—so faithful and true!

Joyfully You teach me the proper path, even when I go astray. Keep showing me Your path and lead me into the best decision. Your perfection and faithfulness are my bodyguards, for You are my hope. I trust in You as my only protection.

God, I believe the plans You have for me are for good and not for disaster, to give me a future and a hope. I am Your own handiwork, Your workmanship, recreated in Christ Jesus. I am born anew to do those good works You planned for me. I take paths which You prepared ahead of time for me, so I may live the good life You lovingly prepared for me. In Jesus' name I pray, amen.

SCRIPTURE REFERENCES

Psalm 25 TPT • Jeremiah 29:11 NLT • Ephesians 2:10 AMPC
Ephesians 5:13 AMPC • Ephesians 1:18 AMPC • John 8:36 NKJV

God's Direction

FATHER-GOD, I am Your child, and You are my heavenly Father. I trust in You completely, and I do not rely on my own opinions. With all my heart, I rely on You to guide me and lead me in every decision I make. I choose to pursue an intimate relationship with You in whatever I do and walk in your perfect will my entire life. I don't think for a moment that I know it all, for wisdom comes when I adore You with undivided devotion and avoid everything that's wrong.

The plans of the mind and orderly thinking belong to me, but from You, Lord, comes the wise answer of the tongue. You weigh the very thoughts and intents of my heart. Today, I choose to roll my works upon You. You will cause my thoughts to become agreeable to Your will, and so shall my plans be established and succeed. You even make everything to accommodate itself and contribute to its own end and Your own purpose.

Today, I choose to let my heart be always guided by the peace of the Anointed One, for You have called me to peace as part of Your one body. I will always be thankful! I will let the Word of Christ live in me richly, flooding me with all wisdom. I pray that every activity of my life and every word that comes from my lips will be drenched with the beauty of my Lord Jesus Christ. In the name of Jesus, I pray, amen.

SCRIPTURE REFERENCES

Proverbs 3:5-7 TPT • Proverbs 16:1-5 AMPC • Colossians 3:10-17 TPT

Praise: Your Banner Over Me Is Love

FATHER, I praise You for delivering and drawing me to Yourself out of the control and the dominion of darkness and transferring me into the kingdom of the Son of Your love.

I am accepted in the beloved. In Your love You chose me for Yourself as Your own before the foundation of the world. Father-God, You caused the One who didn't know sin to be sin for my sake so that through Him I could become the righteousness of God.

I am Yours, and You are mine—Your banner over me is love! Amen.

SCRIPTURE REFERENCES

Colossians 1:13 AMPC • Ephesians 1:4
Song of Solomon 6:3, 2:4 AMPC

Testimony

'I Bought into the Lie That I Was Stupid'

By Rick Renner

WHEN I was a young man, the devil did his best to hijack me by feeding me lies, but I will share how God set me free from oppression and mental strongholds. But first, I need to lay groundwork by expounding on the classic text of 2 Corinthians 10:4: "For the weapons of our warfare are not carnal, but mighty through God to the pulling down of strongholds."

The Greek word *strongholds* is translated from a word that describes a fortress, castle, or citadel. It pictures a stronghold with walls fortified to keep outsiders out. At the same time, it depicts a dreadful prison constructed deep inside a fortress intended to prevent a prisoner from escaping. Thus, a stronghold is a place of captivity and incarceration.

In a spiritual sense, a stronghold is any lie a person believes that imprisons him. The enemy strategically presented me with lie on top of lie—each another brick in the stronghold wall. This mental and emotional prison held me hostage to imaginations with no basis in reality.

Growing up, I never enjoyed sports, yet sports dominated the landscape of my life. Softball, basketball, football, and bowling were a regular part of our family and church life. My father's favorite pastime was fishing, but I had no interest in it either. These activities seemed like drudgery and a waste of time. I was different from the other guys and drawn like a magnet to symphonies, museums, and oil painting.

I was clearly programmed differently, and over time, the devil used that difference to attack my mind and tell me something was wrong. The enemy capitalized on this disparity and fed me a barrage of thoughts like, *What's wrong with you? Why are you such a freak?*

Then in seventh grade, I got sick and missed about half a year of school. When I returned, I was so far behind I had no idea what my teachers were talking about. If someone had taken time to help me, I'm sure I could have caught up, but no one did. The devil seized that vulnerable moment to fill me with inferiority, and thoughts swirled and raged in my mind. The enemy told me over and over, *You're just stupid!*

By ninth grade, my algebra teacher nicknamed me "Stupid" and called me that every day in front of the entire class. On top of all this, I tested poorly on a job-placement exam. When the job counselors called me in to discuss my performance, they told me to never attempt higher education because I was not mentally equipped for it. "Learn how to use a shovel or pour concrete," they said. "Manual labor is all you're cut out for."

There is nothing wrong with doing manual labor, but I felt I had no choice! I was too stupid to do anything else. The enemy was using these negative experiences to fire lies at my mind from every angle. He used classmates and people in authority to hammer into me the message that I was mentally inferior. The fact that I already felt like a misfit compared to other guys who liked sports and fishing convinced me to believe the thoughts Satan was feeding me. Slowly, I bought into the lie that I was inferior, defective, and stupid.

I vividly recall standing in front of my bathroom mirror berating myself: *You are stupid, stupid, stupid! Why can't you understand anything the teacher tells you? Everything about you is wrong. You're not like other guys. You're a misfit and hopelessly STUPID!*

In reality, I'm sure there was nothing wrong with me academically that a good teacher and some encouragement couldn't have fixed, but that help never manifested. The enemy's goal was not just to knock me down or even to keep me down but to trample and destroy me. His objective was annihilation. Looking back, I can just imagine him licking his chops in anticipation of leaving me dead, empty, and completely useless because of the lie I believed about myself.

But before the devil accomplished his goal, God moved in my life, and I was gloriously baptized in the Holy Spirit. That powerful encounter set me free!

My friend, the devil is aware that God has a good plan for your life. He is terrified you will fulfill it, and he'll do his best to stop you. As he did with me, he will try to inundate your mind with lies to keep you from reaching your God-given potential. But you don't have to live behind such mental and emotional prison bars any longer. God's power will enable you to break any oppression or stronghold that has tried to dominate your life!

But wait...Paul added something important in 2 Corinthians 10:4. He said, "For the weapons of our warfare are not carnal, but mighty through God to the pulling down of strong holds."

The words *pulling down* are a translation of a Greek word that means to take down or to disassemble, if needed, bit by bit or piece by piece. It can also be translated to demolish, destroy, dismantle, or throw down. It carries such force that it means to knock down, break up, pull apart, and take to pieces until nothing is left standing.

The words *pulling down* mean if you will latch hold of the power of God and the spiritual weapons God provides, you can pull down any lying stronghold trying to imprison you. But to walk free you must firmly decide not to permit the devil to dominate your mind and emotions any longer. Choose to grab hold of God's power and let it knock down, break up, and tear apart, bit-by-bit if needed, any hint of oppression or strongholds exerting themselves in your life.

I am a living testimony that any person can walk free! And friend, if I could walk free from years of oppression and the strongholds that ruled my younger mental and emotional life, you can walk free too!

Rick Renner is a well-known leader and teacher within the global Christian community. In 1991, he founded and now pastors the Moscow Good News Church in Russia. Rick, a seasoned student of the Greek language, is also a prolific author of more than 30 books. He and his wife, Denise, founded Media Mir, the first Christian television network in the former U.S.S.R. that today broadcasts to a potential audience of 110 million people. Since 2019, Renner TV has broadcasted daily in the U.S. on more than 19 networks.

Testimony

Take Back Your Thought Life

By Eddie Turner

My battle with anxiety began when I was a child. Though I was raised in a loving Christian environment, nervousness and worry were traits that were tolerated and not seen as an enemy in our home. In fact, we assumed that if you really loved someone, you would worry about them. I never knew that worry was a form of fear and that fear is a major cause of mental anguish and torment.

Being raised in a strict Pentecostal tradition, I was continually taught that holiness was always manifested in our clothing attire and the length of our hair. My forefathers meant well, and their desire to separate from worldliness and ungodliness had great intentions, but their emphasis always seem to be one sided. I like to say it this way: I was taught what to wear and where to go, but I never remember anyone teaching me what to think. It wasn't until I was in my late 20s and pastoring a small little church in Tennessee that the protection of my thought life became a reality in my life.

One day as I was driving down the highway on the way to a pastoral visit, a rogue, tormenting thought popped into my mind completely out of the blue. The thought pierced me like a knife, *You must be demon possessed.*

I had never had that thought before and had no idea where that thought came from or why it crossed my mind. I remember the sting of the thought but quickly was able to kick it out and laugh it off. Within two weeks, that same tormenting thought pierced my mind again: *You are demon possessed!* This time the pain was more intense, and I was not able to laugh it off or quickly get my mind on something else. The agonizing thought lingered for a few minutes.

Within three months, that one thought, *You are demon possessed!* had me in its grasp. I couldn't get it out of mind. I tried to reason it away. I tried to pray it away, but it was unrelenting in its torment.

Over the next few months, that one harassing thought materialized into a fear that held me a prisoner in my home. Sleep escaped me. My eyesight became dim, and concentration was almost impossible.

My grandmother died in a mental institution, as they were referred to during that time, and mental instability ran in my family. Growing up, I viewed my relatives as weak and unspiritual and couldn't understand why they couldn't get control of "their nerves." But by the age of twenty-nine, that tormenting spirit invaded my life, and within a few months, I was paralyzed.

Fear, nervousness, anxiety, panic attacks, racing thoughts, continual headaches, insomnia, and sweating plagued me. The inability to concentrate and remember simple things escaped me, and I was convinced I was losing my mind. I was going crazy.

During the next twelve months, through dramatic spiritual encounters with Jesus Christ and things I learned from the Word of God, I discovered that the Lord has given His children the authority to live above anxiety and depression. Though anxiety and depression may run in your family, its tormenting anguish can stop with *you.*

Learning to pray God's Word daily started the renewal of my mind from the toxicity of fear and negativity that I lived with all my life. Praying the Word of God transformed my thinking and set me on a path of freedom and peace of mind.

Our thoughts are blueprints for actions. As we reprogram our minds to think in line with God's Word, our prayer life and thought life will begin to wonderfully change.

You can live above anxiety and fear. You can enjoy the peace that passes all understanding, even when the circumstances of life turn against you. You can recapture your mind. God has promised you a sound mind—a mind that is revived, delivered, and rescued from the negativity and heaviness of a fallen world.

I encourage you to decide to take back your thought life. Daily pray God's promises of power, love, and a sound mind (2 Tim. 1:7). You can't outthink the devil, but by praying and speaking God's Word, you can chase those anxiety-filled thoughts away.

Eddie Turner now travels the world telling his story and sharing powerful principles to help people live above mental chaos and enjoy the peace of mind God promises. Eddie is the author of *Conquering the Chaos in Your Mind* and serves as a teaching pastor and life coach. He and his wife, Amanda, reside in Cookeville, Tennessee.

Anxiety

So here's what I've learned through it all: Leave all your cares and ***anxieties*** *at the feet of the Lord, and measureless grace will strengthen you.*

Psalm 55:22 TPT

Free of Anxiety and Without a Care

Meditation

YOU are here for such a time as this! You are God's child, created and fashioned by Him, and He has an assignment for you. You are free to choose life or death, blessing or cursing! Satan came along with another plan for your life, BUT GOD! The Prayer Therapy in this book will set you free from anxiety, shame, and self-doubt. The choice is yours.

Too many Christians camp out beside the pool of Bethesda. They want to be "fixed," but they are waiting for someone else to change and make them feel comfortable. My friend, it's time to stand up and walk into the water of deliverance and healing! Whether you believe it or not, begin to say to yourself: If it is to be, it is up to me. Nothing determines your choices except *you*.

There was a time that I didn't know there were choices that only I could make, even though it's obvious from the Scriptures that each of us are given the option to choose life or choose death. Over the years, I have learned that God created us to be proactive under the leadership of the Holy Spirit, renew our minds, know God, and become more like Jesus. He created us as three-dimensional beings: spirit, soul, and body. As we mature, we realize all three are connected.

Yet, too often Christians are passive about their own deliverance. They believe if they pray all the right prayers, follow all the right scriptural steps, and say all the correct words, then God will do the rest. But *you* also have an important role in overcoming depression and anxiety. Second Peter 1:5 says, "...You must do your utmost from your side..." (PHILLIPS).

When a feeling of anxiety comes, find a quiet place and ask the Holy Spirit to locate the source. Look at feelings of shame, guilt, and anxiety as opportunities to learn and grow in the grace and knowledge of Jesus Christ."[27]

Let today be the day you choose to apply prayer therapy to your life!

In our humanness we bury painful memories. And yet, you may have forgotten a past that has not forgotten you. Unfortunately, we try to bury shame, self-condemnation, self-rejection, and anything painful. But in those moments, when we least expect it, one of those unacknowledged negative mindsets come roaring back.

God has created you to heal emotionally and grow spiritually. Maturing spiritually is a lifelong process! You have the power and ability to apply prayer therapy, which prepares you to act. You will not walk away from these scriptural prayers and forget who you are in Christ Jesus. The Holy Spirit will imprint the Word on the tablets of your heart and mind.

Worry is probably the major cause of sickness. I will share with you my true-life experiences of emotional healing and spiritual growth. I let go of holding others in judgment and forgave them. The Holy Spirit taught me to cast all my burdens on the Lord during a crucial time in my life. The Holy Spirit taught me how to take off my cares and lay them on the Lord. I approached God boldly in prayer and read His Word aloud to myself until worry subsided. Today I teach classes on overcoming worry, but I find that some Christians are determined to worry and have their anxiety attacks.

The choice is yours. You can lug around the worries and cares, or you can talk to the Lord about any situation—a financial matter, a marriage relationship, the death of a loved one, or children gone astray. Problems come to all, but you must *choose* to cast the care of any circumstance causing you to worry over on the Lord because He cares for you.

---

27 2 Peter 3:18

Prayer

Heavenly Father, Thank You for Your goodness and for welcoming me into Your presence. In the name of Jesus, I cast the whole of my care—all anxieties, worries, and concerns—upon You. I know that You love me and care for me, and those for whom I am praying. Today, I make all my requests known to You with thanksgiving. I know You hear me, and I believe Your best answers are on the way from the moment I ask.

Father, I choose to live out the message I have heard. I set my gaze deeply into the perfecting law of liberty, and I am fascinated by and respond to the truth I hear. I am strengthened by it, experiencing Your blessing in all that I do. Because I love You, my Lord and God, I choose to guard my words. I submit to You and pray to make a difference in the lives of others, and I refuse to be corrupted by the world's values. In the name of Jesus, amen.

SCRIPTURE REFERENCES

Psalm 136:1 • Philippians 4:6 • 1 Peter 5:7 • James 1:23-27 TPT

Deliverance from Hidden Sources of Anxiety

Meditation

Sitting by the window in my music room, I closed my eyes after asking the Holy Spirit to teach me how to wait before the Throne of Grace. A forgotten memory resurfaced and shame, anxiety, and humiliation washed over me accompanied by unwanted resentment toward my mother. There was no fear, only sadness. I knew my mother loved me, and I loved my mother. I also held her in judgment and blamed her for one of the most humiliating days of my life.

Unfolding in my mind was everything that happened that day. As a recent high school graduate, I walked into a new world where people were dressed in business attire. My anxiety level was high, and the moment I opened the door, humiliation quickly moved in. Plastering a smile on my face, I looked for a place to hide from "mocking" eyes.

I wondered how my mother could have done this to me. A skilled seamstress, my mother had created a beautiful, pink-ruffled dress just for me.

From my mother's perspective, she always loved me and wanted the best for me. Appearances were important to her, and even though the dress was inappropriate for a business environment, it was a dress created with love for her daughter. My mother had never been to a business office, and she didn't know what expected attire was; she just wanted me to look "pretty." That was the last ruffled dress I ever wore!

"We are all born into our different situations and bodies which experience unique challenges and forms of suffering. We are born into a world of darkness, blind to our original identity, *so that* we might see the light of God within us. That's why we are here. It's the primary purpose of our lives. So then, we can rejoice in all our of our trials because they are designed to help us experience the light within us! Indeed, all of our struggles give us the opportunity to see the truth of who we are with new eyes rather than languish in victimhood, blame, offense, and judgment."[28]

Prayer

Father, thank You for loving me. Your training of my life is the evidence of Your faithful love, and when You draw me to Yourself, it proves that I am Your delightful child. You forgive my hidden flaws whenever You find them.

Keep cleansing me, God, and keep me from my secret, selfish sins; may they never rule over me! Thank You for freeing me from these faults and rebellion. May the words of my mouth, my meditation, thoughts, and every movement of my heart be always pure and pleasing, acceptable before Your eyes, my only Redeemer, my Protector-God.

Father, enlighten my heart and mind. Help sift and analyze the thoughts and purposes of my heart. I refuse to be a prisoner to anxieties, memories, imagination, or anything else, that would bring me torment. I refute arguments and theories and reasonings and every proud and lofty thing that sets itself up against the true knowledge of God.

In Jesus' name, I lead every thought and purpose away captive into the obedience of Christ (the Messiah, the Anointed One). We use our powerful God-tools for smashing warped philosophies, tearing down barriers erected against the truth of God, fitting every loose thought and emotion and impulse into the structure of life shaped by Christ.

SCRIPTURE REFERENCES

Hebrews 12:6 TPT • Psalm 19:12-14 TPT
2 Corinthians 10:4-5 AMPC, MSG • Hebrews 4:12 AMPC

28 *The Way of Love,* Ted Dekker, pg. 63

A New Imagination of Goodness

Meditation

YOUR teenager is out on his motorcycle while it is raining. He is late, and your imagination is running wild! You imagine him lying in a ditch while cars zoom past him. You are sad and worried, filled with fear, because no one comes to his rescue. Before you realize it, your imagination has him in a casket with the family standing around in shock. Feelings of anxiety have you wringing your hands and pacing the floor. You can't even pray or think of a scripture. You need a new imagination!

One night when our son, David, was late coming home my imagination ran wild as I paced the floor. A strong suggestion surpassed the fear: *You can walk the floor reading your Bible!* Gasping, I reached for my Bible, turned to Psalm 91 and began reading it aloud over David. I don't know how many times I read it before anxiety disappeared. After I had gone back to bed, I heard the front door open, and the hall light was turned off. David was home. You can resist vain imaginations and develop a new imagination full of safety, goodness, and blessing!

Prayer

Father-God, forgive me for entertaining lying vanities that have become strongholds of worry and anxiety in my life. Holy Spirit, I receive You as my divine Counselor and Companion. I have tried to overcome these feelings and incorrect perceptions. I humble myself and ask You to reveal the origin of these feelings and thoughts of anxiety and worry and heal those broken places in my soul caused by past events.

As I renew my mind, I renounce fear of the unknown and receive the healing that You provide. Fill me with light, truth, peace, and wisdom. I receive and thank You for Your forgiveness. I allowed incorrect perceptions to dominate my thinking, and now my mind is renewed by Your Word. I ask You for grace to trust You more and receive the peace that passes understanding. In the name of Jesus, amen.

SCRIPTURE REFERENCES

2 Corinthians 10:3-5 • 1 Peter 5:6-7 • Jonah 2:8

Protected by God All-Powerful

Meditation

Let me encourage you to not only focus on the powerful words in this psalm but to meditate on the imagery as well. You also may want to include your family and loved ones in this prayer of safety.

Prayer

Father, sometimes it seems easier to depress than deal with personal issues, but I come before You today affirming that I sit enthroned under the shadow of Shaddai. You are the God of the Mountain, God the Destroyer of Enemies, God the Self-Sufficient One, God the Nurturer of Babies, and God the Almighty.[29] I am hidden in the strength of You, God Most High. You are the hope that holds me and the stronghold to shelter me, the only God for me, and You are my great confidence.

I do not have to submit to anxiety attacks because You rescue me from every hidden trap of the enemy, and You will protect me from false accusation and any deadly curse or poisoned arrows. Your massive arms are wrapped around me, protecting me. I can run under Your covering of majesty and hide. Your arms of faithfulness are a shield keeping me from harm.

I will never worry about an attack of demonic forces at night nor fear a spirit of darkness of depression and anxiety coming against me. I resist the temptation to be afraid. Your protection and faithfulness are my bodyguards. Evil can't get close to me. Harm can't get through the door.

---

29 TPT Psalm 91:1 Shaddai (*šadday*) is taken from a Hebrew root word with many expressive meanings. It can mean "God of the Mountain, God the Destroyer of Enemies, God the Self-Sufficient One, God the Nurturer of Babies, God the Almighty."

Those who go to God Most High for safety will be protected by God All-Powerful.

You are my hope, and I trust in You as my only protection. This I pray in the name of Jesus.

SCRIPTURE REFERENCES

Psalm 91:1-6 TPT, ICB, MSG • Psalm 25:21 TPT

'Don't Panic! I'm with You!'

When anxiety was great within me, You brought me joy! "Don't panic! I'm with you!" You said. "There's no need to fear for I'm your God. I'll give you strength. I'll help you. I'll hold you steady, keep a firm grip on you" (Isaiah 41:10 MSG). O how I rejoice at those words!

Father-God, I will not yield to fear, for You are always near!

You infuse me with Your strength, and You help me in every situation. Praise You! You hold me firmly in Your victorious right hand. The minute I say, "I'm slipping, I'm falling," Your love takes my hand and holds me. When I am upset and beside myself, You calm me down and cheer me up.

I won't get rattled and lost in despair. I trust You. I praise Your name.

Who would dare tangle with You by messing with one of Your chosen? Who would dare even to point a finger? The One who died for me—who was raised to life for me!—is in the presence of God at this very moment sticking up for me. Do you think anyone is going to be able to drive a wedge between me and Christ's love for me? There is no way! Not trouble, not hard times, not hatred, not hunger, not homelessness, not bullying threats, not backstabbing, not even the worst sins listed in Scripture.

None of this fazes me because Jesus loves me! I'm absolutely convinced that nothing—nothing living or dead, angelic or demonic, today or tomorrow, high or low, thinkable or unthinkable—absolutely *nothing* can get between me and God's love because of the way that Jesus our Master has embraced all of us.

I love You, dear Father, and I shout Your praises. You're so good to me!

SCRIPTURE REFERENCES

Isaiah 41:10 MSG • Psalm 94:19 MSG, NLT, TPT, TLB, NIV
John 14:1 MSG, Voice • Romans 8:38-39 MSG

Anxious for Nothing

FATHER-GOD, I bow low here in Your awesome presence and submit to You. Turn Your searching gaze into my heart and examine me through and through. Find out everything that may be hidden within me. Put me to the test and sift through all my anxious cares. See if there is any path of pain I'm walking on, and lead me back to Your glorious, everlasting ways—the path that brings me back to You.

Boldly and confidently, I pour out all my worries and stress upon You. I choose to leave them with You, for You always tenderly care for me! Empowered by the Holy Spirit, I will be well balanced and always alert because my enemy, the devil, roams around incessantly, like a roaring lion looking for his prey to devour. I'm taking a decisive stand against him and resist his every attack of anxiety with strong, vigorous faith, in the name of Jesus.

SCRIPTURE REFERENCES

Psalm 139:23-24 TPT • 1 Peter 5:6-9 TPT

To Rejoice in the Lord *Always*

FATHER-GOD, no matter how I feel and no matter the cloud of anxiety and depression that swirl around me today, I recognize this is the day the You have made. I choose to rejoice and be glad in it! I rejoice in You always. And, again, I say rejoice. I delight myself in You, and happy am I because You are my Lord!

Father, thank You for loving me and rejoicing over me with joy. Hallelujah! I am redeemed. I come with singing, and everlasting joy is upon my head. I obtain joy and gladness—sorrow and sighing flee away. The spirit of rejoicing, joy, and laughter is my heritage. Where the Spirit of the Lord is, there is liberty—freedom and emancipation from bondage. I walk in that liberty.

Father, I praise You with joyful lips. I am ever filled and stimulated with the Holy Spirit. I speak out in psalms and hymns and make melody with all my heart to You, Lord. My happy heart is a good medicine, and my cheerful mind works healing. The light in my eyes rejoices the hearts of others. I have a good report. My countenance radiates the joy of the Lord.

Father, I thank You that I bear much prayer fruit. I ask in Jesus' name, and I will receive, so that my joy, gladness, and delight may be full, complete, and overflowing. The joy of the Lord is my *strength*. Therefore, I count it all joy, all strength, when I encounter tests or trials of any sort because I am strong in You, Father.

I have the *victory* in the name of Jesus. Satan is under my feet. I am not moved by adverse circumstances. I have been made the righteousness of God in Christ Jesus. I dwell in the kingdom of God and have peace and joy in the Holy Spirit! Praise the Lord! In Jesus' name I pray, amen.

SCRIPTURE REFERENCES

Psalm 118:24 • Philippians 4:8 • Philippians 4:4 • Proverbs 15:13
Philippians 3:1 • John 15:7-8 • Psalm 144:15 • John 16:23 • Zephaniah 3:17
Nehemiah 8:10 • Isaiah 51:11 • James 1:2 • 2 Corinthians 3:17
Ephesians 6:10 • James 1:25 • 1 John 5:4 • Psalm 63:5 • Ephesians 1:22
Ephesians 5:18-19 • 2 Corinthians 5:7 • Proverbs 17:22 • 2 Corinthians 5:21
Proverbs 15:30 • Romans 14:17

No More Gloom and Doom

DEAR Father, thank You for rescuing me out of the doom and gloom of Satan's kingdom and bringing me into the kingdom of Your dear Son. Jesus Christ bought and paid for my freedom and liberty, and I refuse any anxiety or depression that would once again cage me and put me in bondage.

God rescued me from dead-end alleys and dark dungeons. His Son got us out of the pit we were in and got rid of the sins we were doomed to keep repeating. No more tyrannical rule! Now, I live and move and have my being in Him. God in me!

As I live this new life, I will be strengthened from God's boundless resources, so that I find myself able to pass through any experience and endure it with courage. I will even be able to thank God in the midst of pain and distress because I am privileged to share the lot of those who are living in the light.

Father of glory, I pray You would impart to me the riches of the Spirit of wisdom and the Spirit of revelation so that I may know the Lord Jesus Christ through deepening intimacy with Him. I will grow in the knowledge of You and be flooded with light so I understand the confident hope and rich and glorious inheritance You have given to me. I pray to grasp the immensity of this glorious way of life You have for Your followers—oh, the utter extravagance of Your work in us who trust You—endless energy, boundless strength!

SCRIPTURE REFERENCES

Colossians 1:11-14 TLB, PHILLIPS, MSG, TPT • Acts 17:28
Ephesians 1:17-19 NLT, TPT, MSG

Chin Up!

FATHER, here I am again feeling anxious. Yet, I totally trust You to rescue me one more time so that I can see once again how good You are. Here's what I've learned through it all: I will not give up; I will not be impatient; I am entwined as one with You, my Lord and God. Therefore, I choose to be brave and courageous and never lose hope. Yes. I choose to keep on waiting—for You will never disappoint me!

LORD, I bow down before Your divine presence and bring You my deepest worship as I experience Your tender love and Your living truth. For the promises of Your Word and fame of Your name have been magnified about all else! At the very moment I called out to You, You answered me! You strengthened me deep within my soul and breathed fresh courage into me. By Your mighty power I can walk through any devastation, and You will keep me alive, reviving me. Your power set me free from fear and anxiety.

You keep every promise You have ever made to me! Since Your love for me is constant and endless, I ask You, LORD, to finish every good thing that You have begun in me. I trust You to perfect everything which concerns me! (Ps. 138:8 AMPC). You have said, "...[I will] not, [I will] not, [I will] not in any degree leave you helpless nor forsake nor let [you] down (relax My hold on you)! [Assuredly not!]" (Heb. 13:5 AMPC). No, You will not in any way fail me nor give me up nor leave me without support. You will not in any degree let me down or relax Your hold on me! You're always with me, ready to help, so I can be fearless no matter what!

I've got my chin up! My head is held high, dear God, because I'm looking to You!

SCRIPTURE REFERENCES

Psalm 27:13-14 TPT • Psalm 138 TPT • Hebrews 13:5 AMPC • Psalm 25:1-2 MSG

Praise: Unquestionably Free!

FATHER, I praise You for welcoming me into Your house and covering me by Your covenant of mercy and love. You have set me free, and I am Your true son/daughter. I am unquestionably free!

I am free to choose life, and now You are my exceeding great joy. You have made me glad! I praise You for breaking open my life and freeing me from my chains of worry and harassing thoughts. Hallelujah!

SCRIPTURE REFERENCES

Psalm 5:7-7-8 TPT • John 8:36 TPT • Psalm 119:16-17 TPT • Psalm 5:11 TPT

Testimony

Stalked by Anxiety

By Max Davis

I CANNOT say that I've struggled with depression, but deep pain, anxiety, and fear have stalked me. I've experienced betrayal at the deepest level, encountered loss, and watched my disabled child suffer. Yet, at the same time, I've experienced incredible peace and joy. Second Corinthians 8:2 says, "In the midst of a very severe trial, their overwhelming joy...welled up..." (NIV). Is it even possible that joy can well up in a severe trial? Is it possible to experience joy in the midst of undue stress or anxiety? *Yes!* It is possible because Jesus is really risen. And because Jesus is risen, He is fully present with us, even when our circumstances and feelings scream the opposite.

Paul said, "If our hope in Christ is for this life alone, we are to be pitied more than all men. But Christ has indeed been raised from the dead" (1 Cor. 15:19-20 BSB). Paul made that statement because he experienced great suffering after becoming a believer. Yet, he also experienced great comfort because he knew Jesus was risen. That's why Paul also wrote, "Blessed be the God...of all comfort, who comforts us in all our tribulation, that we may be able to comfort those who are in any trouble, with the comfort with which we ourselves are comforted by God" (2 Cor. 1:3-4 NKJV). Psalm 16:11 says, "...in your [God's] presence there is fullness of joy..." (AMPC).

After Jesus rose from the grave and ascended, He promised to send the Comforter, the Holy Spirit. That's why Paul—as well as all believers today—have Jesus' presence inside us via the Holy Spirit. The Comforter truly comforts us and gives us fullness of joy in the midst of whatever we are going through. Personally, I have experienced His tangible, supernatural peace that passes all understanding and, believe it or not, a joy that calms my anxious mind.

Max Davis is the author of more than 35 books, including *Jesus, Josiah, & Me: How My Supernatural Encounter with an Autistic Boy Revealed the Wonder of God's Presence*. He and his wife, Alana, make their home in Baton Rouge, Louisiana.

Testimony

Out of the Shadows

By Chandler Grace McCollum

THE valley of the shadow of death is a terrifying place to wander alone. It is lonely, and your worst fear is lurking around every corner. No matter what you do you cannot seem to find the light to guide you out of the shadows. The valley is littered with footprints, making it hard to navigate until you open your eyes to the deception that there is no escape. It is a miserable place to reside; however, I have spent a good amount of my short life in the shadow of depression.

My first battle with the shadows began when the day after I turned 13. We were forced to move from Florida to my grandparent's house in Georgia. I thank the Lord every day for my grandparents because if they had not taken us in, we would have been homeless. My entire world was flipped upside down in 24 hours. We moved away from everything and everyone I knew and loved dearly, and to top it off, that move marked the beginning of the end of my parent's relationship.

I was an extremely hurt and angry teenager for most of my eighth-grade year. As I got more involved in my church, the shadows began to lift. I found happiness in my small group and a few friends I made at my new school. I was happy—briefly. My freshman year of high school my grandparents' house caught on fire, and I lost my entire friend group that

I had placed my identity in. The shadows began to creep back in. My sophomore year of high school marks my greatest battle with depression. I have never felt more alone than I did that year, and I truly believed that it was my fault I was alone. I began to self-harm as I gave into the lies that the enemy was feeding me. Things began to look up as I had found a new friend group. But everything was not as it seemed, and it quickly fell apart. My parents were also fighting constantly, and I realized that we would never truly be a family again.

Then one night in the middle of a major breakdown, my mother said something that truly snapped me out of my mindset. She told me that depression is selfish. I am sure I stared at her with my mouth open for a moment, unable to believe what she had just said to me.

I am not a selfish person, I thought. *I have always gone above and beyond for family and friends, almost to a fault.* But my mother told me to consider what I was constantly meditating on, and so I did. The thoughts that filled my head were all about *me.* They were about how **I** could not do anything right, how **I** was messed up, how **I** was not enough, etc. These thoughts were all the bad things I had been told about myself and truly believed, whether they were true or not. The common denominator in all those terrible thoughts was "**I.**" I could hardly believe it, but I was being selfish—not in my actions but in my thoughts.

I also came to realize that being selfish in your thoughts eventually does translate to being selfish in your actions as well. Being so focused on your own inability inhibits you from using your love and talents to glorify the One who loves you unconditionally.

My mother's tough love was just what I needed. Since then, I have never truly fallen as far into depression as I did my sophomore year of high school. That does not mean that I never struggled with depression again. The shadows attempted to take over again when my mother was told that my father had a son, who was just under a year old. My parents were not divorced yet, and my father had managed to hide it from us for almost a year. He probably would have hidden it longer had the woman he had the child with not called my mom to tell her. This event would have been my breaking point if my mother had not made me reconsider my mindset. To me, it was the ultimate betrayal as I felt totally rejected by my father. In my head, at the time, I believed that we were not good enough for him, so he went off and started a "better" family.

Depression remains an ongoing battle for me, and I believe it will be a continual battle as the enemy attempts to silence my light, my words. It is very hard to see God working in and around you when you reside in the valley of the shadow of death. And yet, we cannot be blind to the One who loves us most even though the shadows tempt us to feel alone and lost.

Until you decide for yourself to not be a victim of your circumstances, it is nearly impossible to find your way out of the valley. Until you change your mindset, which is much easier said than done, you will continue to be blinded by the shadows. The enemy desperately wants you to be focused on yourself and your inability. When stuck in a place of self-hate, it is hard to truly love those around you and show them the love of our amazing heavenly Father. The enemy wants you in a place of self-denial. He wants you to be blind to who you truly are supposed to be, your true potential.

A journey out of the shadows all begins when you choose to be blinded no longer and take one step into His Light.

Chandler Grace McCollum, the granddaughter of Germaine Copeland, is a young wife and mother whose heart was softened by her sweet boy. She is the author of *Silver Linings—Short Stories and Poems of Growth*.

Depression

Arise [from the ***depression*** *and prostration in which circumstances have kept you—rise to a new life]! Shine (be radiant with the glory of the Lord), for your light has come, and the glory of the Lord has risen upon you!*

Isaiah 60:1 AMPC

Fresh Courage

Meditation

THE Bible is my favorite book, and the primary reason is that God and His Word are One. We get to know Him through the pages of the Bible and through prayer. Another reason I love it so much is that I find the answers to real-life situations in its pages. Listen to this: "Anxiety in the heart of man causes depression but a good word makes it glad."[30] The Bible is full of good words.

The years of depression that followed me was the result of lies I believed about something that happened when I was a child. I share my testimony in more detail on page 216.

But let me say now that depression is for most people built lie upon lie upon lie.

In fact, this stronghold of depression exalts itself above the knowledge of God in fierce battle for your soul, a battle for the focus of your mind. Too often, we look for a pill to make us happy, to help us cope with this complex world we live in. Antidepressants may or may not help you, but there is not an antidepressant that will cure you. (There also may be serious side effects to consider.)

But today, I can offer you a way to reconnect with the One who loves you unconditionally and can deliver you unquestionably.

I offer you prayer therapy that will expose those mindsets that separate you from the sweet presence of God. Are you ready to enjoy the good and abundant life God designed for you?[31] There are side effects: grace, love, peace, and joy. You can exchange the garment of heaviness for the

30 Proverbs 12:25

31 Ephesians 2:10 AMPC, John 10:10

garment of joy! "A joyful heart is good medicine, but depression drains one's strength" (Prov. 17:22 GW).

Prayer

Father-God, thank You for delivering me from depression and opening my eyes to see the miracle-wonders hidden in Your Word. Once I was blind, but now I can see. LORD, I love Your commandments. You have given me life because of Your unfailing love. The very essence of Your Word is truth, and all Your just regulations will stand forever.

Thank You for the truth-giving Spirit that unveils the reality of every truth within me. There is nothing in the universe that has the power to separate me from Your endless Love. Depression has been exposed and stripped of its power to oppress or control my thoughts.

Today, I know the truth; I choose to continue in Your Word, and the Truth sets me free.

You keep every promise You have ever made to me! Since your love for me is constant and endless, I ask You, Lord, to finish every good thing that You have begun in me! At the very moment I called out to You, You answered me! By Your mighty power, I can walk through any devastation, and You will keep me alive, reviving me. You strengthen me deep within my soul and breathe fresh courage into me. It's all in the name of Jesus!

SCRIPTURE REFERENCES

Psalm 119:18-19, 159-160 TPT • John 16:12-14 TPT
Romans 8:35 • Psalm 138:3, 7-8 TPT

Arise!

FATHER-GOD, I ask myself, Why am I down in the dumps, my dear soul? Why am I crying the blues? I will no longer. I will choose to fix my eyes on God and begin praising again. I have plenty of reason to praise You, Father, for all You do for me. Despite all my emotions, I will believe and praise You—the One who saves me! You are my help! You put a smile on my face. You are *MY GOD.*

Father, as I look truly and carefully around me, I see that darkness blankets the earth; people all over are cloaked and sunken in darkness. But Father, Your Word says that You arise and shine on me. So I arise! I put my face in the sunlight, for Your light has broken through!

God, You have done everything You promised, and I'm thanking You with all my heart.

You pulled me from the brink of death, my feet from the cliff-edge of doom. You keep my feet from stumbling so I can walk before You bathed in life-giving light. I stroll at leisure with You in the sunlit fields of life.

SCRIPTURE REFERENCES

Isaiah 60:1-2 Voice, MSG, TPT • Psalm 42:11 MSG, TLB, Voice
Psalm 56:13 TLB, MSG, Voice, TPT

Deliverance from Depression

Dear Father, thank You for delivering me from the weight of oppression and lifting me up above the pain of depression and shame. Satan intended it for my destruction, but You set boundaries around me and determined my appointed time in history.

It is through You that I live and function and have my identity. My lineage comes from You. In the same way I have received Jesus as my Lord and Messiah by faith, I continue my journey of faith, progressing further into my union with You. I rejoice because my spiritual roots go deeply into Your life as I am continually infused with strength, encouraged in every way.

Jesus, I am established in the faith that I have absorbed, and I will forever be enriched by my devotion to You. You have not abandoned me. You have given me life, and I have come alive! Today, I know that I am in You, and You are living in me!

When my soul is in the dumps, I rehearse everything I know of You! Then You promise to love me all day and sing songs all through the night! My life is Your prayer.

SCRIPTURE REFERENCES

Acts 17:26-28 TPT • Colossians 2:6-7 TPT • John 14:19-20
Psalm 42:6-8 MSG

When Praise Goes Up, Walls Come Down

Meditation

"Picture this: *It's midnight.* ***In the darkness of their cell,*** *Paul and Silas—**after surviving the severe beating—aren't moaning and groaning**; they're praying and singing hymns to God. The prisoners **in adjoining cells are wide awake,** listening to them pray and sing. Suddenly the ground begins to shake, and the prison foundations begin to crack. You can hear the sound of jangling chains and the squeak of cell doors opening. Every prisoner realizes that his chains have come unfastened"* (Acts 16:25-26, VOICE).

God spoke to Joshua, "Look sharp now. I've already given Jericho to you, along with its king and its elite forces. Here's what you are to do: March around the city, all your soldiers. Circle the city once. Repeat this for six days. Have seven priests carry seven ram's horn trumpets in front of the Chest. On the seventh day march around the city seven times, the priests blowing away on the trumpets. And then, a long blast on the ram's horn—when you hear that, all the people are to shout at the top of their lungs. The city wall will collapse at once. All the people are to enter, every man straight on in" (Joshua 6:2-5, MSG).

BOTH these passages above help us to see that when trouble comes our way, our mouths need to be open praising God. As we praise our way through trouble, the chains fall off and the walls come down!

Prayer

Dear Father,

There are times when I feel attacked, chained, and trapped by my own thoughts that bully and harass me. But when they come to defeat me, I know what to do! I will praise You in every moment *through every situation*. I don't give thanks *for* everything but *in* everything. Whenever I speak, my words will always praise You. I will always be joyful and always keep on praying. No matter what happens, I will always be thankful, for this is Your will for all who belong to Christ Jesus. My life itself is a prayer and a praise!

In Jesus' name and through Your Word, I destroy every proud obstacle that keeps me from walking in Your light. I capture rebellious thoughts and teach them to obey You, Jesus Christ, my Lord and Savior. The weapons of the war I fight are not of this world but are powered by God and effective at tearing down the strongholds erected against His truth. I demolish every high-and-mighty philosophy that pits itself against the knowledge of You, the one true God. I'm taking prisoners of *every thought, every emotion,* and subduing them into obedience to Jesus, the Anointed One.

Your strength shall be my song of joy. At each and every sunrise, my lyrics of Your love will fill the air! For You have been my glory-fortress, a stronghold in my day of distress. My Savior, I sing with joy the lyrics of Your faithful love for me! You are a safe place for me—a good place to hide. Strong God, I can always count on you!

I continually offer to God a sacrifice of praise—the fruit of my lips—that give thanks to Your name. I no longer must offer up a steady stream of blood sacrifices as in the Old Covenant, but through Jesus, I will offer up to You a steady stream of praise sacrifices. These are "the lambs" I offer from my lips to celebrate Your name! In Jesus' name, I praise, amen.

SCRIPTURE REFERENCES

Psalm 34:1 Voice • 1 Thessalonians 5:16-18 TLB, MSG, TPT
2 Corinthians 10:4-5 Voice, NLT • Psalm 59:16-17 TPT, MSG
Hebrews 13:15 TPT, PHILLIPS

God My Deliverer

FATHER-GOD, You knew me before You formed me in the womb. You knew me before I was born. You consecrated me and appointed me for Your purpose and Your plan. Before I saw the light of day, You had holy plans for me. No longer can depression separate me from You. Old things have passed away, and behold, all things have become new!

You have become my exceeding great joy. My heart is overflowing with praise to You, my Lord! My soul is full of joy because You are my God and my Savior and my Deliverer. You noticed me, and You have satisfied my hunger with good things.

My passion is to know Jesus. I continually long to know the wonders of Jesus more fully and experience the overflowing power of His resurrection working in me. I am one with Him in His sufferings and in His death. I am experiencing complete oneness with Him in His resurrection from the realm of death. I am in Christ, and therefore, I have passed from death to life!

SCRIPTURE REFERENCES

Jeremiah 1:4-5 ESV, MSG • 2 Corinthians 5:17 • Psalm 43:3 AMPC
Luke 2:53 PHILLIPS • Philippians 3:9-11 TPT

A Praise Song to You

All glory to the Father, all glory to the Son, all glory to the Holy Spirit—the great Three-in-One! Here I am in Your presence to offer up the sacrifice of praise! I was a sinner hiding from You, but now I know that You were always present. I was blind to the light of truth, and depression separated me from You. I didn't realize that You are the One I was waiting for, yet I waited and waited and waited for You.

You lifted me out of the ditch, pulled me from deep mud. You stood me up on a solid rock to make sure I wouldn't slip. You taught me how to sing the latest God-song, a praise-song to You—the Great Three-in-One! More and more people are seeing this: they enter the mystery, abandoning themselves to You.

Here on earth I do not have a city that lasts forever, but I am looking for the city that I and my fellow travelers will have in the future. Through Jesus I choose to always offer to You my sacrifice of praise, coming from lips that speak Your name. With the help of the Holy Spirit, I choose to do good to others, and share with them, because such sacrifices please You, my loving heavenly Father.

SCRIPTURE REFERENCES

Psalm 40:1-3 MSG • Hebrews 13:14-16 NCV

My Helmet of Salvation

LORD, You know everything there is to know about me. You perceive every movement of my heart and soul, and You understand my every thought before it even enters my mind. You are intimately aware of me, Lord. You read my heart like an open book, and you know all the words I'm about to speak before I even start a sentence!

By the power of the name that is above every name, I refuse to be depressed, and I let go of anything that would keep me down. Father-God, You have set before me life and death, and I choose life and give the Spirit control of my mind that leads to life and peace.

Christ's resurrection is my resurrection too. I yearn for all that is above and fill my thoughts with heavenly realities, not with the distractions here on earth. I renew my mind with the precious Word of God. Your Word is full of living power. It is as sharp as a surgeon's scalpel, cutting through everything, whether doubt or defense, laying us open to listen and obey.

I take the helmet of salvation and walk confidently in the powerful reality of who I am in Christ Jesus, my Lord. Whatever may come, I face the adversary clothed in the full armor of God. I choose to study and meditate on the Word of God until it writes sweet peace on the tablets of my heart and mind.

SCRIPTURE REFERENCES

Psalm 139:1-3 TPT • Hebrews 4:12 TLB, MSG • Romans 8:5-6 NLT
Colossians 3:1-4 TPT • Ephesians 6:17

No More 'Diet of Tears'

DEAR Father, right now I'm overwhelmed by my sorrow and pain. I can't stop feasting on my tears. I've been on a diet of tears—tears for breakfast, tears for supper. But, Father, despite all my emotions, I will believe and praise You who saves me and is my life!

You are a shelter for those who know misery. You are my Refuge and my High Tower. You are my Stronghold in times of trouble. I lean on You and confidently put my trust in You. I praise You, God.

Lord, You lift me up when I am bowed down. I choose to be strong and take courage in You. I am built solid and grounded in righteousness, far from any trouble—nothing to fear! Far from terror—it won't even come close!

My mind is stayed on You! I stop allowing myself to be agitated and disturbed and intimidated and cowardly and unsettled. I give the devil no room to work. People with their minds set on You, You keep completely whole, steady on their feet, because they keep at it and don't quit. I depend on You and keep at it because in You I have a sure thing. Perfect, absolute peace surrounds my imaginations because I am consumed with You and confidently trust in You.

In the name of Jesus, I loose my mind from wrong thought patterns. I tear down strongholds that have protected bad perceptions and critical opinions about myself. I submit to You, Father, and resist fear, discouragement, self-pity, and depression. I will not give place to the devil by harboring resentment and holding onto anger. I surround myself with songs and shouts of deliverance from depression, and I will continue to be an overcomer by the word of my testimony and the blood of the Lamb.

You strengthen those who are discouraged and energize those who feel defeated.

You say to the anxious and fearful, "Be strong and never afraid. Look, here comes your God! He is breaking through to give you victory!" (Isa. 35:3-4 TPT).

Father, I thank You that I have been given a spirit of mighty power, love, self-control, and a calm and well-balanced mind. I have the mind of Christ and hold the thoughts, feelings, and purposes of Your heart. I have a fresh mental and spiritual attitude, for I am constantly renewed in the spirit of my mind with Your Word, Father.

Therefore, I brace up and reinvigorate and cut through and make firm and straight paths for my feet—safe and upright and happy paths that go in the right direction. I arise from depression. In Jesus' name, I rise to new life. I shine, and I am radiant with the glory of the Lord. I refuse to be dejected and sad, for the joy of the Lord is my strength! Hallelujah! Amen.

SCRIPTURE REFERENCES

Psalm 9:9-10 Voice, AMPC • Ephesians 4:27 Voice
Psalm 42:3, 5, 11 MSG, Voice • Psalm 146:8 • 2 Timothy 1:7 TPT, AMPC
Isaiah 35:3-4 TPT • Isaiah 54:14 MSG, TPT • Ephesians 4:23-24 AMPC
Hebrews 12:12-13 AMPC • Jeremiah 29:11-13 AMPC • Isaiah 60:1 AMPC
Isaiah 26:3 MSG, TPT • John 14:27 AMPC • Nehemiah 8:10 NLT

Dark Dungeons of Depression Gone

Meditation

Moses returned to the Lord and said, "O Lord, why have you brought trouble upon this people? Is this why you sent me? Ever since I went to Pharaoh to speak in your name, he has brought trouble upon this people, and you have not rescued your people at all" (Exod. 5:22-23 NIV).

In this passage, Moses is discouraged and complaining to God, but we can take a lesson from his honesty and humility. I believe that too often we fear making a negative confession as we approach the Father, sometimes crossing the line of honesty into denial and delusion. But let's be honest. God already knows what we are feeling. He can handle our anger, complaints, and disappointments. He understands us. He is aware of our human frailties (Ps. 103:14), and He can be touched with the feelings of our infirmities (Heb. 4:15). Whether your "trouble" is a business failure, abandonment, depression, mental disorder, chemical imbalance, oppression, a marriage problem, a son or daughter who has strayed away from God and in a strange land of drugs and alcohol, financial disaster, or anything else, the following prayer is for you.

Sometimes when you are in the midst of discouragement, it is difficult to remember that you have ever known any scripture. But let me encourage and admonish you to read this prayer aloud until you recognize the reality of God's Word in your spirit, soul, and body. Remember, God is watching over His Word to perform it (Jer. 1:12 AMPC). And He will perfect that which concerns you (Ps. 138:8).

Prayer

Lord, I have been surrounded and battered by troubles. I am pressed on every side by troubles but not crushed. I am perplexed but not driven to despair. I may get knocked down, but I am not destroyed. I am not sure what to do, but we know that You know what to do! You have not left my side.

I have exhausted all my possibilities for changing my situation and circumstances and have found that I am powerless to change. But while all things are not possible with man, all things are possible with You. Therefore, I humble myself before You, confident You will lift me up.

I have a great High Priest who has gone through the heavens: Jesus Your Son. And I hold firmly to the faith I profess. My High Priest is able to sympathize with my weaknesses. He was tempted in every way, just as I am—yet without sin. I approach Your throne of grace with confidence, so that I may receive mercy and find grace to help me in my time of need.

In spite of these feelings—discouragement, depression, and anger—I choose to believe that Your word to Moses is Your word to me. You are mighty to deliver, Father-God! Because of Your mighty hand, You will drive out the forces that have set themselves up against me. You are the Lord, Yahweh, the Promise-Keeper, the Almighty One. You appeared to Abraham, to Isaac, and to Jacob and established Your covenant with them. You brought the Israelites out of Egypt with might miracles and a powerful hand. You did great and awesome miracles before the Egyptians.

And now, Father, I believe You hear my cries. I will live to see Your promises of deliverance fulfilled in my life. Not one word has failed of all Your wonderful promises to us. You are a Covenant-Keeper!

Jesus Christ has set me free to live a free life. So, I take my stand! Never again will I let anyone or anything put a harness of slavery on me. I stubbornly refuse to go back into the bondage of ___________ . You freed me from being a slave! You have rescued me! You have liberated me from oppression and depression.

You are my Father, and You love me. You have delivered me out of the darkness and gloom of Satan's kingdom and brought me into the kingdom of Your dear Son. No more dead-end alleys and dark dungeons. You have delivered me into the kingdom of the Son You love so much, the Son who got us out of the pit we were in, got rid of the sins we were doomed to keep repeating. You have rescued us completely from the tyrannical rule of darkness.

You are my Father, and You love me. You have delivered me from the past that has held me in bondage and translated me into the kingdom of love, peace, joy, and righteousness. I will no longer settle for the pain of the past. Where sin abounds, grace does much more abound.

Father, what You have promised, I will possess in the name of Jesus. I strip off every weight that slows me down, especially the sin that so easily trips me up, and I run with endurance the race God has set before me. I rebuke the spirit of fear, for I am built solid and grounded in righteousness. Oppression and destruction shall not come near me. I am more than a conqueror through You who loved me. Overwhelming victory is mine through You, in Jesus' name I pray, amen.

SCRIPTURE REFERENCES

2 Corinthians 4:8-9 NLT, MSG • Mark 9:24 NLT • Galatians 5:1 MSG, TPT
John 4:19 • Deuteronomy 26:8 • Luke 18:27
Colossians 1:13-14 MSG, TPT, TLB • 1 Peter 5:6 NIV • Romans 5:20
Hebrews 4:14-16 NIV • Exodus 6:3-4 NLT, Voice
Hebrews 12:1 AMPC • Isaiah 54:14-16 MSG • 1 Kings 8:56 NLT
Romans 8:37 NKJV, NLT • Exodus 5:22-23 • Exodus 6:1-11

My House of Peace

FATHER, thank You for every spiritual blessing in the heavenly realm that has already been lavished upon me as a love gift from You, my wonderful heavenly Father, the Father of our Lord Jesus, all because You see me wrapped into Christ. This is why I celebrate Jesus with all my heart!

I choose to walk in the lavish blessing of peace. Through skillful and godly wisdom is my house (my life, my home, my family) built, and by understanding it is established on a sound and good foundation. By knowledge shall its chambers of every area be filled with all precious and pleasant riches—great priceless treasure. My heart is filled with the treasures of wisdom and the pleasures of spiritual wealth in the name of Jesus.

My house of peace is securely built. It is founded on a rock—revelation knowledge of Your Word, Father. Jesus is my Cornerstone. Jesus is Lord of my household. Jesus is my Lord—spirit, soul, and body. And the house of the uncompromisingly righteous shall stand.

In my house, we love each other with the Godkind of love, and we dwell in peace. My home is deposited into Your charge, entrusted to Your protection and care. Father, as for me and my house, we will serve the Lord, in Jesus' name. Hallelujah! Amen.

SCRIPTURE REFERENCES

Ephesians 1:3 TPT • Proverbs 24:3-4 AMPC, TPT • Proverbs 12:7 AMPC
Colossians 3:14-15 AMPC • Acts 20:32 AMPC • Luke 6:48 AMPC
Joshua 24:15 NLT • Acts 4:11 TPT

Praise: Smuggled into Your Secret Place

FATHER, my Creator, I choose to praise You! I shout praises to You because You cherish me constantly in Your every thought!

You are my shelter! You smuggled me into Your secret place where I'm kept safe and secure—out of the reach of depression. I am triumphant now over depression, and I offer You praise, singing, and shouting with ecstatic joy! Today, I shout praise to You, my Lord!

SCRIPTURE REFERENCES

Psalm 139:17-18 TPT • Psalm 27:5-6 TPT

Testimony

Set Free from 28 Years of Depression and Addictions

By David W. Copeland

I AM no stranger to depression and anxiety. For 28 years, my unresolved issues and unmet needs drove me to addictions that controlled my life and almost cost me my life. During these 28 years, I struggled with bouts of depression, suicidal thoughts, obsessive compulsive thoughts, and anxiety. I looked for love and peace in all the wrong places, using drugs and alcohol to fill the emptiness inside. While the highs brought me brief escapes from emotional pain, they always took more than they gave me.

I began my journey of addictions at the age of 14 when I was first introduced to pornography. The next year I got high from smoking marijuana for the first time and felt a false freedom from feeling unloved, rejected, and abandoned. A lot of these feelings started when I was two years old, and I thought that I had been replaced by my newborn sister. At age 16, I was so lost and depressed that I tried to kill myself. By age 18, I was thoroughly hooked on drugs, trying to numb my feelings and anxiety and silence obsessive compulsive-thinking.

You name it, I tried it—marijuana, cocaine, meth, heroin, uppers, downers. From ages 17 to 26, I dealt drugs, worked a full-time job, got married, and had three children. Five years after the birth of my fourth child, I had the opportunity to get into business for myself. That business grew into a six-figure income and led me down a deep, dark hole that I couldn't get out of for years. My daily routine became getting my work crews off to work, cocaine or meth in the morning, and going to strip clubs. My life became about getting high in the morning and during the day and then at night drinking to take the edge off. I would get drunk and high so I could do whatever came next.

But the reality of my destructive lifestyle smacked me right in the face on May 29, 1999. Despite repeated warnings from my attorney not to drink and drive, I started driving again while drinking. Trying to get to my dope man, I got arrested for my fourth DUI (driving under the influence). This arrest triggered many things, and I was finally arrested on possession of a firearm by a convicted felon. At that point, I faced multiple charges, two felonies, and a few misdemeanor charges in three counties.

By December 1999, I was taken out of the jail system and put in the prison system where I was no longer in control of anything in my life. There is a huge difference between jail and prison. In February 2000, I entered Walker State Prison, and thick steel doors slammed shut behind me.

Could it get any worse? Yes. My childhood sweetheart who became my wife of 24 years came to the prison to tell me that she and my children were divorcing me. This only confirmed the thought that brought all the pain from the beginning—I was unlovable and being rejected and abandoned again. I didn't know any other way to deal with the pain, so I left that visitation and went straight to the prison dope man and started taking downers again.

God spoke to me three times in the early part of 1999, and He told me if I didn't quit what I was doing, I would lose everything. Now, I had lost everything. In May 2000, while sitting on bunk #69 in dorm 5, I heard God say in an audible voice, "Choose this day life or death. It is up to you!"

I chose life. After 28 years of trying everything this world had to offer, a peace I had never known flooded me. Although I was born again at age 10, the path I chose at 16 led me to this point in my life. I opened my locker, cleared out all the pornography, and threw it in the trash where it belonged. I read the Bible every spare minute I had because I wanted to get to know this Jesus who died for me and my heavenly Father who loved me unconditionally. My Poppa, as I have come to know Him, loves me through everything. I eventually joined a prison prayer group, where we saw my Father perform miracle after miracle as we prayed for His will to be done in situations.

While in prison, I was learning to make bathtub-sized batches of crystal meth that would be worth a small fortune on the outside, but I turned my back on it all and never looked back. No amount of money could rival the newfound peace in my heart. For the first time in my life, I felt loved and accepted by the Creator of heaven and earth. He alone filled my heart with the peace I had searched so hard to find.

Did I do something that brought about this miraculous conversion? Yes, I did. I made the choice to walk in the light. And it was the prayers of my mom and all those God sent alongside of her to pray for me to hear clearly from God and know I had to make a choice. The first scripture the Holy Spirit gave my mom for me was this: "All your spiritual children shall be disciples taught by the Lord and obedient to His will, and great shall be the peace and undisturbed composure of your children" (Isa. 54:13 AMPC). She also prayed the eyes of my understanding would be flooded with light (Eph. 1:18 AMPC) and my ears would be open to Him (John 10:27-28 TPT). God did the rest!

To get out of prison, I needed a place to live and a job. My dad told me that I could come live with them, and my mom gave me a job filing papers at the ministry. Today, I serve as Vice President of Prayers That Avail Much Ministries, reaching millions around the world with the power of prayer. I realize that I am actually the "poster child" of radically effective and life-altering scriptural prayer.

God is continually speaking to those who have walked away from Him or are yet to find Him. God is speaking to you and your loved ones right now. That is how much He loves you. God did not just speak to me that one time in Walker State Prison, but that day I *heard* Him. I heard Him because my mother prayed my spiritual ears and eyes open. God is no respecter of persons, and He will answer your prayers just the same.

Even now, I still choose life several times a day. What does that mean? It means when depression and anxiety try to steal my peace, I choose life by choosing what I will think on. I choose to replace every thought that attacks my peace with what God's Word says. I put on worship music, the Scriptures, and prayers to hear all day long if necessary. I pray scripture-based prayers aloud because it builds my faith (Rom. 10:17) and renews my mind (Rom. 12:1-2). One of my favorite prayers is "To Rejoice in the Lord *Always*," found on page 88.

This book is filled with scriptural prayers that will pull you from the deep, dark hole of depression and anxiety and fill you with the peace that God promises you. But you must choose to pray the prayers, choose to listen to the Word of God, and choose to allow the Holy Spirit to strengthen you. There are some times in our lives that are easier than others, but we should always choose LIFE!

David W. Copeland, Germaine Copeland's son, has served as Vice President of Prayers That Avail Much Ministries since 2011. He has four adult children, a growing number of grandchildren, and his first great grandchild. David makes his home in Monroe, Georgia.

Testimony

A Mother's Prayers That Availed Much

By Germaine Copeland

WHEN the Holy Spirit began to teach me to pray for David, I thought all my prayers would be focused on David. After all, he was the problem—he was the one who needed to get his act together. My mind was focused on getting David off drugs and through school. But I soon learned that addiction is a family problem.

Lord, teach me to pray! Knowing that God's Word is His will, I started a search in Strong's Concordance to find out what He said about children. I had confidence that if I asked according to His will, He would hear me, and I knew that when He heard me that He would grant the petition that I desired of Him.[32] I was eager to pen a prayer of petition to present to the Father.

In my research, Isaiah 54:13 jumped off the page: "And all your [spiritual] children shall be disciples [taught by the Lord and obedient to His will,] and great shall be the peace and undisturbed composure of your children (AMPC)."

Knowing I had heard from God, I wrote my very first scriptural prayer. "David Wayne Copeland is a disciple taught of the Lord and obedient to God's will, and great shall be his peace and undisturbed composure."

32 1 John 5:14-15

The next Sunday at church someone passed me a note. *"While praying for your son, God gave me this scripture!"* It was Isaiah 54:13! Despite others trying to talk me out of it, I knew that I had heard from God.

Still focusing on David, I ignored "taught of the Lord" and emphasized "David is obedient to God's will." For years I wrote "sermonettes" for him, and at the drop of a hat, I preached many messages to him. God probably breathed a sigh of relief when I finally realized He was David's teacher—not me! I know David did, and I felt as though a weight had been lifted from my shoulders.

Of course, I was expecting all my prayers to be about David, but God had something else in mind. At times, when I sat down to pray certain scriptural prayers, the Holy Spirit used the prayers to turn His spotlight on *me!* I'm not sure why I was so surprised because I had been blaming myself for David's wrong decisions.

One morning, feeling holy I sat down for my meeting with God. He talked to me through the pages of the Bible, and I talked to Him. As I was enjoying the moment, a thought wiggled its way into my mind: *I can't think of a single sin in my life.* My smug, joyous attitude soon crumbled.

I was reading Matthew 18 when a scene from the past Sunday morning rudely interrupted my quiet time. From the depths of my soul, and I saw and heard the words I said to my family as we drove home from church. I explained to them where our pastor had been wrong! My husband tried to stop me by asking me how I could possibly know more than a man who had been studying and preaching for years? Indignantly, I answered that I had revelation knowledge!

Honestly, I tried to reason with the Holy Spirit before I repented. After all, our pastor was not a "little one" (Matt. 18:1-6 AMPC), so what did this scripture have to do with what I had said? I melted into a puddle of tears as the Father exposed my judgmental and critical attitude toward our pastor who is His valued son. Furthermore, the words I had spoken to my family could cause my children to stumble and sin.

This was the beginning of an adventure in spiritual growth and emotional healing that continues until this day. I am empowered by the instruction and correction "giving me the strength to take the right direction and lead me deeper into the path of godliness."[33]

Emotions are real and can be overwhelming! I continued learning by trial and error. At times I beat myself up—where had I failed—how could this happen to one of my children—there was soul searching!

There were times I thought David had set out to prove my prayers would not work. So, I went on the warpath to deliver him from the strange land of addictions. I screamed at the devil. I bound. I loosed. I loosed, and I bound. I rebuked! Nothing was working!

I was so angry one day that I was ready to turn David over to Satan for the destruction of his flesh and the salvation of his soul. When I told my prayer partner, Doris, she fell to the floor and cried out for God to forgive me for speaking those words.[34]

The truth is, there is absolutely nothing God's power cannot accomplish. He has given knowledge and understanding to others who have walked the road before us. I studied books on addictions and attended group sessions where I gained insight into family dynamics. The Holy Spirit exposed and analyzed soulish areas of my life that needed to be transformed—an unexpected blessing even though at the time it was trying. David was God's son, and I could not walk the journey they were walking together.

The Holy Spirit and I got my motive aligned with His, and I saw the intercession of Jesus is about eternal purposes. His desires for David became my desires. When my emotions would attempt to overwhelm me, I spoke God's Word over David. Over time, God revealed the hurt and pain that David carried. I asked him to forgive me for mistakes I had made out of ignorance and immaturity.

---

33 2 Timothy 3:16 TPT

34 James 1:29

The Holy Spirit began to reveal the prayer that Jesus was praying for David, his son. "Father, Satan desires to have David, that he may sift him as wheat, but I pray that His faith will not fail him, and when he is converted, he will strengthen his brethren."[35] God has answered this prayer.

God taught me to pray His will, which is His Word. He loved David before the foundation of the world, and I learned to separate soulish prayers from Spirit-led prayers. Praise God, for all He taught me about family dynamics—nothing is as important as our relationships with Him, our family and friends. We all are in the school of the Spirit, where we are learning to walk in the light of God's love. This is where we are trained to respect one another and forgive one another as God has forgiven us.

The last written prayer that I prayed for David before His deliverance was adapted from a prayer in Liberty Savard's book, *Breaking Your Strongholds.* The following are excerpts of the prayer I prayed for him:

"In the name of Jesus, I bind David's body, soul, and spirit to the will and purposes of God for his life. I bind his mind, will, and emotions to the will of God. I bind him to the truth and to the blood of Jesus and his mind to the mind of Christ. I bind his feet to the paths of righteousness. I bind him to the work of the cross with all its mercy, grace, love, and forgiveness.

I loose every old, wrong, ungodly mindset, attitude, idea, desire, belief, motivation, and every wrong mind/body agreement he has about wrong behaviors. I tear down, crush, smash, and destroy every stronghold associated with these things. I loose any stronghold in his life that has been justifying and protecting hard feelings against anyone.

In the name of Jesus, I loose the power and effects of any harsh or hard words (word curses) spoken to, about, or by David. I loose all effects and bondages from him that may have been caused by mistakes I have made.

---

35 Luke 22:31-32

I bind and loose these things in Jesus' name. He has given me the keys and the authority to do so. Thank You, Lord, for the truth. Amen."

Hurt, Grief & Guilt

When someone is ***hurting*** *or* ***brokenhearted,***
the Eternal moves in close and revives
him in his pain.

Psalm 34:18 VOICE

Therefore, now no ***condemnation*** *awaits*
those who are living in Jesus the Anointed,
the Liberating King.

Romans 8:1 VOICE

Healing for the Brokenhearted

Father, I haven't yet acquired the absolute fullness that I'm pursuing, but I run with passion into Your abundance so I may reach the purpose You have called me to fulfill and want me to discover. I desire to forget the past and fasten my heart to the future instead. I run straight for the divine invitation of reaching the heavenly goal and gaining the victory-prize through the anointing of Jesus.

Lord, my heart has been crushed by pain, and I ask You to save me from the pain of a past that has not forgotten me. Jesus, I choose to forgive those who have caused me emotional pain, and I submit to the anointing upon You to be hope for the poor, freedom for the brokenhearted, new eyes for the blind, and so much more.

Forgive me for holding onto grievances that blinded me to a love that holds no record of wrong. Father, I choose to bind my mind to the love of God that breaks the power of a victim mentality and translates me into complete freedom.

Today, I choose to bring all my grievances into the light of forgiveness and wholeness. I forgive others as Christ has forgiven me! I have been crucified with Christ. It is no longer I who lives, but Christ lives in me. The life which I now live in the flesh I live by faith in the Son of God, who loved me and gave Himself for me. In Jesus' name I pray, amen.

SCRIPTURE REFERENCES

Philippians 3:12-14 TPT • Psalm 34:17-19 TPT
Luke 4:18-19 TPT • Galatians 2:20 NKJV

Guarding My Heart

Dear Father, deliver me from the fear of human opinion that disables, cripples, and even paralyzes me. Instead, I choose to trust in You knowing You will shield me from the harassment of other people's opinions. People go around making plans and voicing opinions, but You, the Eternal, have the final word. Your thoughts and ways are what matter. They are above and beyond ours.

Holy Spirit, teach me to guard the affections of my heart, for they affect all that I am. Keep me alert to the welfare of my innermost being, for from there flows the wellspring of life. With Your help, I will avoid dishonest speech and pretentious words, and I am free from using perverse words no matter what! I choose to set my gaze on the path before me with fixed purpose, looking straight ahead and ignoring life's distractions.

I watch where I'm going and stick to the path of truth, and the road will be safe and smooth before me. I purpose not to be sidetracked for even a moment and or take the detour that leads to darkness. I choose to pray instead of worrying and let petitions and praises shape my worries into prayer.

I will go out with joy and be led home wrapped in peace. You, dear Father, are my Source of peace.

Before I know it, I experience a sense of God's wholeness, everything coming together for good to settle me down. It's wonderful what happens when You displace worry at the center of my life! In the name of Jesus, amen.

SCRIPTURE REFERENCES

Proverbs 29:25 MSG • Proverbs 4:23-27 TPT • Philippians 4:6-7 MSG
Isaiah 55: 9 Voice • Isaiah 55:12 TPT • Micah 5:5 NLT

Dismantling Guilt

DEAR God, I'm overwhelmed, swamped, and submerged beneath the heavy burden of my guilt. It clings to me and won't let me go. My festering wounds are a witness against me, reminding me of my failure and folly. God, give me mercy from Your fountain of forgiveness!

I know Your abundant love is enough to wash away my guilt. Because Your compassion is so great, take away this shameful guilt of sin. Forgive the full extent of my rebellious ways and erase this deep stain on my conscience.

I choose to freely admit my sins when Your light uncovers them, and You are faithful to forgive me every time. You are just to forgive me my sins because of Jesus Christ, who continues to cleanse me from all unrighteousness.

My completeness is found in Him, and I am completely filled with God as Christ's fullness overflows within me. Jesus, You are the head of every kingdom and authority in the universe! Through my union with You, I have experienced circumcision of the heart. All the guilt and power of sins has been cut away and is now extinct because of what You have accomplished for me. Thank You that Your will is done in my life! In the name of Jesus, amen.

SCRIPTURE REFERENCES

Psalm 38:4-5 TPT • Psalm 51:1-2 TPT • 1 John 1:8-9 TPT
Colossians 2:10-11 TPT

Forgive Me!

FATHER-GOD, You gave me the Living Word, which is full of energy and pierces more sharply than a two-edged sword. It even penetrates to the core of my being where soul and spirit, bone and marrow meet. Your Word interprets and reveals the true thoughts and secret motives of my heart. By your words I can see where I'm going. They throw a beam of light on my dark path.

Today, I choose to come clean and ask You to forgive me for trying to hide my sins from You. I am ready to finally admit the sins I had buried because I was afraid. Like a confused and frightened child, I was afraid of being punished.

Now I come to the mercy set where You established a new covenant with Your blood, and I receive forgiveness for my sins—my wrong motives, wrong perceptions, and ungodly, judgmental, and critical attitudes toward others.

Thank You for loving me and exposing those issues that opened the door for self-condemnation. To You, my life-giving God, I openly acknowledged my evil actions. And You forgave me! All at once the guilt of my sin is washed away, and all my pain has disappeared. Thank You for rescuing me completely from the tyrannical rule of darkness and translating me into the kingdom realm of Your beloved Son.

For in Jesus all my sins are canceled, and I have the release of redemption through Jesus' blood. In His mighty name, I pray, amen.

SCRIPTURE REFERENCES

Hebrews 4:12 TPT • Hebrews 12:24 TPT • Psalm 32:5 TPT
Colossians 1:13-14 TPT • Psalm 119:105 MSG

Freedom from Shame

DEAR heavenly Father, I come to You in Jesus' name. Thank You for the terrible suffering Jesus experienced for me. He took all my shame, and yet, He wants to give me glory.

Thank You, Jesus, my Savior, for becoming my shame in Your suffering. You were sacrificed for me because You love me so much.

I humble myself before You now to believe Your Word and to have faith that I can be free through the blood of Jesus. Your sacrifice is enough for me, and I don't have to hide anymore.

Jesus, You have set me free to hold my head high and become the person You made me to be. I receive my freedom through Your blood. Jesus, Your blood is enough for me.

I am Your child, Father, and I know that is Your will for me. Thank You, dear Father. I love You. I know You hear me. I pray this in the precious name of Jesus, amen.[36]

SCRIPTURE REFERENCES

Ephesians 1 and 2 • James 4:7 • 1 John 3:1 • Matthew 26:28

36 *Redeemed from Shame*, Denise Renner, pg. 61-62

Forgiveness for Abortion

Meditation

Often, I hear from women who carry the guilt and condemnation of a decision they made many years ago. Rather than being a solution, the decision to terminate a pregnancy becomes the beginning of unresolved grief. Abortion often impacts future relationships as women secretly carry the burden of loss and shame. Others deny any negative effects from the abortion. But when any one of His children repents, God is faithful—God is just—and God forgives.

Prayer

Father, in the name of Jesus, I ask You to forgive the sin of our nation for disregarding the sanctity of life and sanctioning abortion. I recognize that You uniquely create each person, Lord. Each one is marvelously made!

You know each person inside and out. You know every bone in the body. All the stages of a life are spread out before You. I value the life You give. Lord, I repent of my sin and the sin of our nation. Be merciful to me, Lord. I ask Your forgiveness, knowing that You are faithful and just to forgive me and cleanse me from all unrighteousness. Amen.

SCRIPTURE REFERENCES

Psalm 139 MSG • 1 John 1:9 NKJV • Matthew 18

Connected to God My Father

Meditation

In 2001, Glenn and Terri Bone, my son-in-law and daughter, presented us with a newly-adopted grandson, Christopher Howard Bone. For the first time, I truly understood the full meaning of adoption. When they brought him home, we could hardly wait to cradle him in our arms. He is our grandson in every way—with all the rights of our other ten grandchildren. It thrills my heart when Christopher says that he has always felt he belonged to both sides of his family. It is so important to know who you are and know you are accepted in God's family.

Prayer

God, I've searched for a place where I would feel connected. So often, I have felt all alone and wondered why I was even born. Today, I believe and know in my heart that it was always in Your perfect plan to adopt me as Your delightful child, through my union with Jesus, the Anointed One, so that Your tremendous love that cascades over me would glorify Your grace—for the same love You have for Your Beloved One, Jesus, You have for me. This unfolding plan brings You great pleasure!

Since I am now joined to Christ, I have been given the treasures of redemption by Jesus' blood—the total cancellation of my sins—all because of the cascading riches of His grace. I did not receive the "spirit of religious duty," leading me back into the fear of never being good enough. I have received the "Spirit of full acceptance," enfolding me into the family.

I will never feel orphaned, for as He arises within me, my spirit joins with His, and I say the words of tender affection, "Beloved Father!" The

Holy Spirit makes Your fatherhood real to me by whispering into my innermost being, "You are God's beloved child!" Thank You for being my beloved Father! In Jesus' name, amen.

SCRIPTURE REFERENCES

Ephesians 1:5-7 TPT • Romans 8:15-16 TPT

Forgiving Others

CLOTHED in Your armor, Father, I choose to forgive anyone who has caused me distress, grief, embarrassment, hurt, financial loss, or pain of any kind. In Jesus' name, I choose to forgive in order that Satan might not outwit me. For I am aware of his schemes.

In fact, everything is falling apart on me, Father-God. Put me together again with Your Word. Let my passion for life be restored, tasting joy in every breakthrough that You bring to me. Hold me close to You with a willing spirit that obeys whatever you say. Then I can show to other guilty ones how loving and merciful You are. They will find their way back home to You and know that You will forgive them. O God, my saving God, deliver me fully from every sin, even the sin that brought bloodguilt. Then my heart will once again be thrilled to sing the passionate songs of joy and deliverance!

Again, I choose to accept life and make a commitment to be patient and tolerant with others, always ready to forgive if I have a difference with anyone. I forgive as freely as You have forgiven me. And, above everything else, I am truly loving, for love binds all the virtues together in perfection. In Jesus' name, amen.

SCRIPTURE REFERENCES

Psalm 51:12-14 TPT • Psalm 119:105 MSG • Colossians 3:12-14
James 4:7 AMPC, PHILLIPS • Psalm 119:107 MSG

Letting Go of Bitterness

Meditation

Many an ex-spouse carries a sense of shame, wondering how the marriage could have failed so miserably. Many of these individuals also have faced injustices and emotional upheavals that create deep hurts and wounds and an anger so near the surface they risk sinking into the trap of bitterness and revenge. Their thoughts may turn inward as they consider the unfairness of the situation they faced and dwell on how badly they've been treated. And for many, the bottom line is anxiety and depression.

In a family divorce situation, bitterness sometimes distorts ideas of what is best for the child/children involved. One parent (and sometimes both parents) will use the child/children against the other. Unresolved anger often moves one marriage partner to hurt the one he or she holds responsible for the hurt and sense of betrayal felt.

But, my friend, there is healing available! There is a way of escape for all who will turn to the Healer, obeying Him and trusting Him.

Prayer

Father, life seems so unjust, so unfair. The pain of rejection is almost more than I can bear. My past relationships have ended in strife, anger, rejection, and separation. Lord, help me to let go of all bitterness and indignation and wrath (passion, rage, bad temper) and resentment (anger, animosity).

You are the One who binds up and heals the brokenhearted and bandages my wounds. I receive Your anointing that destroys every yoke of bondage. I receive emotional healing by faith and thank You for giving me the grace to stand firm until the process is complete. Thank You for wise counselors. I acknowledge the Holy Spirit as my wonderful Counselor. Thank You for helping me work out my salvation with fear and trembling, for it is You, Father, who works in me to will and to act according to Your good purpose.

In the name of Jesus, I choose to forgive those who have wronged me. I purpose to live a life of forgiveness because You have forgiven me. With the help of the Holy Spirit, I get rid of all bitter words, temper tantrums, revenge, profanity, insults, anger, rage, brawling, and slander, along with every form of malice. I desire to be kind and compassionate and affectionate to others, graciously forgiving them, just as in Christ, You forgave me.

With the help of the Holy Spirit, I make every effort to live in peace with everyone and to be everyone's friend. I also make every effort to be holy, for I know that without holiness no one will see You, Lord. I purpose to see to it that I do not miss Your grace. I will keep a sharp eye out for weeds of bitter discontent and try to stay out of quarrels. I watch that no bitter root grows up within me to cause trouble. I will watch and pray that I enter not into temptation or cause others to stumble.

Thank You, Father, that You watch over Your Word to perform it. Your Word says You rise early to keep a promise! And whom the Son has set free is free indeed. I declare that I have overcome resentment and bitterness by the blood of the Lamb and by the word of my testimony. In Jesus' name, amen.

SCRIPTURE REFERENCES

Ephesians 4:31-32 AMPC, TPT • Psalm 147:3 NLT • John 14:26-28
Romans 12:18 • Hebrews 12:14 NIV, TPT • Isaiah 10:27
Jeremiah 1:12 NLT • John 8:36 • Revelation 12:11

Free to Live a Free Life

FATHER, in the name of Jesus, I come to You with guilt and emotional hurt. I confess my transgressions to You, continually unfolding the past till all is told. You are faithful and just to forgive me and to cleanse me of all unrighteousness. You are my Hiding Place, and You, Lord, preserve me from trouble. Your Word is a healing salve to my wounds. You surround me with songs and shouts of deliverance.

You saw me while I was being formed in my mother's womb, and on the authority of Your Word, I was wonderfully made. Now I am Your handiwork, recreated in Christ Jesus. Father, You have delivered me from the spirit of fear. Neither shall I be confounded and depressed.

You gave me beauty for ashes, the oil of joy for mourning, and the garment of praise for the spirit of heaviness that I might be called a tree of righteousness, the planting of the Lord, that You might be glorified. I speak out in psalms, hymns, and spiritual songs, offering praise with my voice and making melody with all my heart to You. Just as David did in 1 Samuel 30:6, I encourage myself in You.

Jesus was put to death because of my misdeeds but raised to secure my acquittal, absolving me from all guilt before You. I've been translated from the kingdom of darkness into the kingdom of light, and therefore, I walk in the light! You anointed Jesus and sent Him to bind up and heal my broken heart and liberate me.

Christ has set me free to live a free life. So I take my stand! Never again will I let anyone—or anything—put a harness of slavery on me. I stand fast in my liberty! Free of sin, heartache, depression, grief, and anything else that would try to diminish my freedom.

In Jesus' name, I choose to forgive all those who have wronged me in any way. My spirit is Your candle, Lord, searching all the inmost parts of my being, and the Holy Spirit leads me into all truth. When reality exposes shame and emotional pain, I remember that the sufferings of this present life are not worth being compared with the glory that is about to be revealed to me and in me and for me and conferred on me!

The chastisement needful to obtain my peace and well-being was upon Jesus, and with the stripes that wounded Him, I was healed and made whole—spirit, soul, and body. And now, I choose to walk above the troubles of this world. I walk in joy and peace and in the abundant life Jesus purchased for me. In Jesus' name I pray, amen.

Scripture References:

Psalm 32:5-7 AMPC • Romans 4:24-25 AMPC • 1 John 1:9
Isaiah 61:1 AMPC • Deuteronomy 30:19 • Galatians 5:1 MSG
Mark 11:25 • Psalm 139:13-16 AMPC • Hebrews 13:5-6 AMPC
Ephesians 2:10 AMPC • Proverbs 20:27 • 2 Timothy 1:7
John 16:13 • Isaiah 54:4 AMPC • Romans 8:18 AMPC • Isaiah 61:3
Isaiah 53:5 AMPC • Ephesians 5:19 AMPC
Romans 5:3-5 AMPC • Colossians 1:13

The Case Is Closed

DEAR Father, I regret things in my past. I'm ashamed and tempted to feel guilty. Then, I read Your Word that says, "So now the case is closed. There remains no accusing voice of condemnation against those who are joined in life-union with Jesus, the Anointed One." How I rejoice over Your Word! I'm so grateful Your Word says when I ask forgiveness You are faithful and just to forgive me and cleanse me from all unrighteousness. I'm grateful You have removed my sins as far as the east is from the west.

Your Word says that You will remember our sins and iniquities no more, which means You have forgotten my actions of the past. Therefore, if You will not remember them, then I will not remember them. I choose to let them go now—once and for all.

The blood of Jesus and the washing of the water by the Word do their cleansing work in my life. With the arrival of Jesus, the Messiah, that fateful dilemma is resolved. Those who enter into Christ's being-here-for-us no longer have to live under a continuous, low-lying black cloud. A new power is in operation. The Spirit of life in Christ, like a strong wind, has magnificently cleared the air, freeing me from a fated lifetime of brutal tyranny at the hands of sin and death. The Son has set me free, so I am truly free!

I'm not saying that I have this all together, that I have it made. But I am well on my way, reaching out for Christ, who has so wondrously reached out for me. Friends, don't get me wrong: By no means do I count myself an expert in all of this, but I've got my eye on the goal, where God is beckoning us onward—to Jesus. I'm off and running, and I'm not turning back. I forget all of the past as I fasten my heart to the future instead. I press on to reach the end of the race and receive the heavenly prize for which God, through Christ Jesus, is calling us. In Jesus' name, amen.

SCRIPTURE REFERENCES

Romans 8:1 Voice, TPT • 1 John 1:9 • Psalm 103:12-14 • Hebrews 8:12
1 John 1:7 • Ephesians 5:26 • John 8:36 NLT
Philippians 3:12-14 MSG, TPT, NLT

The Pain of Grieving

Meditation

Nothing in life can prepare us for the death of a loved one. Whether death results from a sudden accident or a sustained illness, it always catches us off-guard. Death is so deeply personal and stunningly final that nothing can prepare us emotionally for its arrival. With every death, there is a loss. And with every loss, there will be grief.

Grief doesn't come and go in an orderly, confined timeframe. Just when we think the pangs of anguish have stolen their last breath, another wave sweeps in and we are forced to revisit the memories, the pain, the fear. Sometimes we try to resist the demands of grieving. We long to avoid this fierce, yet holy pilgrimage. We fight against the currents, terrified of being overwhelmed, of being discovered, of becoming lost in our brokenness.

Culture tells us to move past this process quickly. Take a few days, weeks perhaps, to grieve, but don't stay there too long. Grieving can make those around us uncomfortable. Friends sometimes don't know what to do with our pain. Loved ones struggle to find adequate words to comfort our aching wounds.

Yet grief, as painful a season as it is, is a necessary part of our healing. To run from grief is to run from the very thing that can quell the pain of our loss. If we come to God and use Bible verses and prayer for healing, our grief has a purpose. Grieving is the process God uses to bring us to a place of wholeness.

Grieving can be the most difficult time for people. Trying to balance the feelings of pain and loss while going forward with your everyday life. Give yourself space and time, be honest with your emotions, don't grieve alone, and don't lose hope. With this collection of Bible verses, we can turn to Scripture for ease and comfort as we look to overcoming grief.

Below you will find a prayer for an individual who is grieving and a prayer for a friend who is grieving. You can also visit biblestudytools.com for a list of Bible verses to help you on the topic of overcoming-grief. They will remind you of God's great love for you and His readiness to help you.

Prayer

Father-God, I come before You on behalf of __________ who is experiencing loss. I celebrate with those who celebrate and weep with ______ who is grieving.

In this time of sorrow, I remember that all praises belong to You, the Father of tender mercy and the God of endless comfort. I am here to support my friend (or family member), and I ask You to comfort ___________ and strengthen him/her at this time of despair and sorrow.

Give him/her a beautiful bouquet in the place of ashes, the oil of joy instead of tears of mourning, and the mantle of joyous praise instead of the spirit of heaviness. LORD, you are _______'s Shepherd, and he/she will have all that is needed. You let this precious child of Yours rest in green meadows, and You lead __________ beside peaceful streams.

Thank You for renewing _______________'s strength and guiding Your child along right paths. Even now as he/she walks through the darkest valley, _________ will not be afraid, for You are close beside him/her. Surely Your goodness and unfailing love will pursue _________ all the days of his/her life, and he/she will live in the house of the LORD forever.

SCRIPTURE REFERENCES

Romans 12:15 TPT • 2 Corinthians 1:3 TPT
Isaiah 61:1-3 TPT • Psalm 23 NLT

Prayer for Overwhelming Personal Grief

Meditation

My friend, when you cannot seem to pray—you simply have no words—the Holy Spirit will help you read this prayer. Perhaps you will speak just a line or two, but it's a beginning. At other times, just open your Bible and read God's Word where you will always find instruction, wisdom, and comfort.

Prayer

Father, I never expected the death of my ______ to be so complex and difficult. There's no one who can heal this pain except You. I feel as though I can't go on, but I know that You are with me. Your rod and staff comfort me. When my emotions overwhelm me and I feel drained of energy, You alone are my Strength. The road ahead seems dark, and sometimes I feel so alone. How long will this sadness weigh me down? How do I get through this time in my life?

Lord, even though my feelings are jumbled up and I don't know what to pray, You know my thoughts. Thank You for the Holy Spirit who is my Comforter, Counselor, Helper, Intercessor, Advocate, Strengthener, and Standby. I am in the valley of the shadow of death, and I've never experienced anything so final. Although I feel so alone, I remember that You will never forsake me and never leave me without support.

I know You are always near. I choose to focus on You, my faithful God. I ask You to infuse me with Your strength and help me in every situation. Hold me firmly with Your victorious right hand.

SCRIPTURE REFERENCES

John 14:16-17 AMPC • Isaiah 41:10 TPT

Getting Past the Past

FATHER, I realize my helplessness in saving myself, and I glory in what Christ Jesus has done for me. I let go—put aside all past sources of my confidence—counting them worth less than nothing, in order that I may experience Christ and become one with Him.

Lord, I have received Your Son, and He has given me the authority (power, privilege, and right) to become Your child.

I unfold my past and put into proper perspective those things that are behind. I have been crucified with Christ, and I no longer live, but Christ lives in me. The life I live in the body, I live by faith in the Son of God, who loved me and gave Himself for me. I trust in You, Lord, with all my heart and lean not on my own understanding. In all my ways I acknowledge You, and You will make my paths straight.

I want to know Christ and the power of His resurrection and the fellowship of sharing in His sufferings, becoming like Him in His death, and so, somehow, to attain to the resurrection from the dead. So, whatever it takes, I will be one who lives in the fresh newness of life of those who are alive from the dead.

I don't mean to say that I am perfect. I haven't learned all I should yet, but I keep working toward that day when I will finally be all that Christ saved me for and wants me to be.

I am bringing all my energies to bear on this one thing: Regardless of my past, I look forward to what lies ahead. I strain to reach the end of the race and receive the prize for which You are calling me up to heaven because of what Christ Jesus did for me. In His name I pray, amen.

SCRIPTURE REFERENCES

Philippians 3:7-9 TLB • Proverbs 3:5-6 NIV • John 1:12 AMPC
Philippians 3:10-11 NIV • Psalm 32:5 AMPC • Romans 6:4
Philippians 3:12-14 TLB • Galatians 2:20 NIV

Forgetting Failure

FATHER, I look to You. Help me learn of You, even in the midst of this adversity and remain strong in You and in Your mighty power.

Father, I believe that You brought me to this point in my life, and I will not be afraid, for You turn into good anything that is intended for my undoing.

You are God, and there is no other; there is none like You. You know the end from the beginning, from ancient times, and what is still to come. Your purpose in this situation will stand, and You will do all that You please.

I refuse to be amazed and bewildered at the fiery ordeal that is taking place to test my quality, as though something strange, unusual, and alien to me and my position were befalling me.

Father, I remember that Your blessing brings wealth, and You add no trouble to it. There is surely a future hope for me, and my hope will not be cut off. I have sown that good might come to others, and I believe that I shall reap in due season, if I faint not.

O, my soul, don't be discouraged. Don't be upset. Expect God to act! For I know that I shall again have plenty of reason to praise Him for all that He will do. He is my help! He is my God!

Lord, I offer up to You sacrifices of praise—the fruit of my lips, which confess Your name—and I will not forget to do good and to share with others, for with such sacrifices You are pleased. In Jesus' name I pray, amen.

SCRIPTURE REFERENCES

Ephesians 6:10 NIV • Proverbs 10:22 NIV • Genesis 50:20 TLB
Proverbs 23:18 NIV • Isaiah 46:8-10 NIV • Galatians 6:9
1 Peter 4:12 AMPC • Hebrews 13:15-16 NIV

Praise: The Oil of Bliss

My Father, I am here to praise You and thank You for wrapping Yourself around me. You are here to heal my broken heart, hurts, grief, and guilt and walk with me through this healing process.

You comfort me in my sorrow and strengthen me when I feel crushed by despair. Thank You for giving me a beautiful bouquet in the place of ashes, the oil of bliss instead of tears, and the mantle of joyous praise!

SCRIPTURE REFERENCES

Isaiah 61:1-3 TPT

Testimony

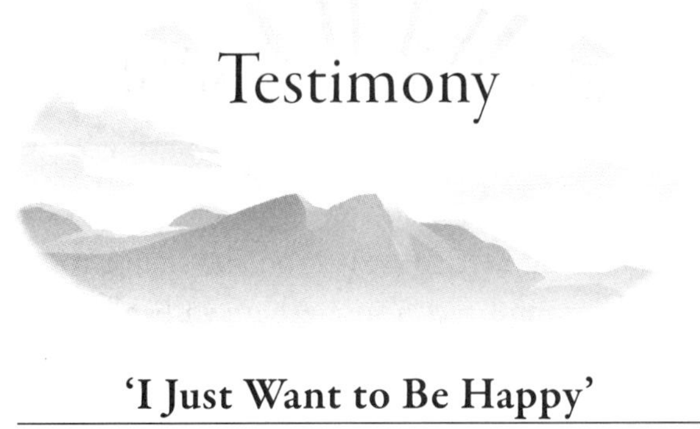

'I Just Want to Be Happy'

By Adrienne Cooley

I THOUGHT when I answered the call to ministry that my life would be filled with people overwhelmed with love aimed right back at me in response to my heartfelt efforts to serve them. Boy, was I mistaken! As a pastor's wife, I quickly came to know that's not always how it goes.

As years passed and life happened like it does for us all, I found myself constantly consumed with thoughts of an intense need to escape and "get away" from it all. It was a slow fade, but my thought processes moved from wanting to go to the beach all the time to actually wishing I were dead. I literally started to think things were just too complicated to overcome and began buying into the lie that the devil loves to feed many of us: "Maybe those I love would be better off without me."

I was focusing on all the wrong things in my life, obviously—the stresses of life, challenges in ministry, broken relationships, disappointments, and betrayal—instead of being thankful for my amazingly beautiful family, health, supportive friends, and wonderful church. You get it! I was a mess and felt hopeless. Ever been there? We all fall into wrong thinking patterns and may not even realize how far we let those negative thoughts take us before we look up and realize we have fallen into depression. I struggled to get out of bed every day for almost a year.

I knew I had to dig deeper into the things of God by intentionally thinking on things that are lovely, pure, and of good report. As we think in our hearts, so are we Scripture tells us. This seemed nearly impossible for me as much as I knew it was the answer. Even if you have never been in a place quite as dark as this, I'm sure you can relate. I prayed that God would open the eyes of my understanding and that I would know again the hope to which He called me, as Ephesians 1:18 says.

God is so faithful. I was able to find some time alone and unload my heart's pain to Him. It is absolutely imperative that we get in the presence of God, surrender our hearts, and cry out to Him. He is where our help comes from! My conversation with Him started like this: "God, what is the point of me being in ministry? So that what? I can help everyone be as miserable as I am? I just want to be happy."

God answered and said, "I want you to be happy."

My reply, "No, You don't! You just want me to have joy, whatever that is!"

So, I did what anyone would do. I googled the word *happy,* and when I did, I found *happy* defined as "enjoying, showing, or being marked by pleasure, satisfaction, or joy." God answered me through His own words as I read the Scriptures. It was like the words *enjoying* and *joy* popped off the screen, and immediately two scriptures came to mind: Psalm 16:11, "In His presence there is *fullness of joy,*" and 1 Timothy 6:17, "God gives us all things *richly to enjoy.*"

In that very moment, I got permission from God to be happy! This was the answer that started my healing process. He gives us joy in His presence so we can enjoy it. That is the definition of happy: *enjoying joy*! For the first time in my life I knew that God cares about our happiness and wants us to not just have joy but to enjoy it! God heard my cries from the bondage of depression and freed me through the hope I found in His Word.

If we hide the Word in our hearts, when we need it most, it will be there and will not return void but accomplish what God sent it forth to accomplish in our lives.

Adrienne Cooley co-pastors Harvest Church with her husband, Kevin, in Mobile, Alabama. She continues her personal testimony in her book *Happy ANYWAY* and shares the secret to a happy, fulfilled life in her second book *Love ANYWAY*.

Testimony

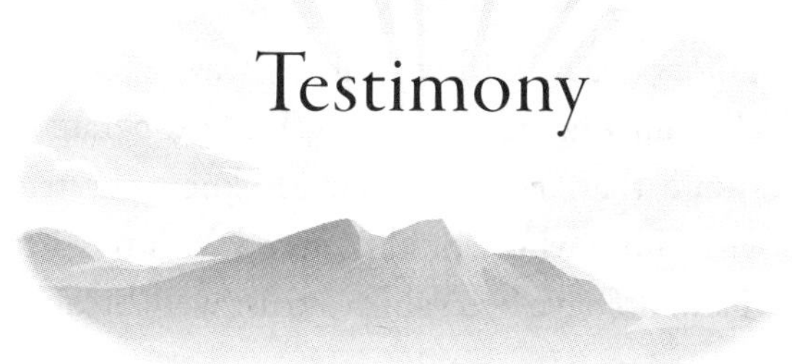

People May Hurt You, But God Never Will

By Kelley Pruett Robinson

FIFTEEN years ago, I thought my life was amazing. I had a position at a church I loved, doing what I loved working with the music/theater department. I was the director of a children's creative arts program that God was blessing exponentially as well as assistant to the director of the adult music department. Life was good, and I was having a blast...until I wasn't.

I woke up one day somewhere between the amazing Christmas program we had completed and upcoming Easter productions unable to breathe. My depleted energy level left me having to choose between a shower that day or eating; doing both was not at option. Brain fog had set in so badly that I felt as though I didn't have two brain cells to rub together. Being the type to beat a dead horse, I tried to keep going, but the more I did, the worse I got.

Within days I had to resign from both positions. It broke my heart. I was admitted to the hospital for test after test, but even after nine days of inpatient testing, there seemed to be no explanation for this debilitation. Friends in other states reached out to help. I finally moved to Virginia to live with a dear friend, who said, "Come on up, and I'll take care of you." And she did. I'll always love her for that.

Meanwhile, rumors began to fly about my leaving. Things that were said hurt dreadfully, but I hadn't the strength to exonerate myself. I just cried out to God and thanked Him that He knew the truth, and He would contend with those who would contend with me. I trusted Him even when those I should have been able to trust were breaking my heart.

About a year after I left, my former roommate called me to let me know that the bathroom off my former bedroom was being retiled, and when they began the demolition, black mold was found behind the walls. I remembered at that moment that during the productions, just prior to my taking ill, I discovered a nasty patch of black mold in the wardrobe room right off my workspace. I had spent much time in that room rooting around for costumes. I did report it, but nothing was done.

I called the doctor who had spent so much time trying to figure out why I was so sick. I told her about the mold, and just like a light had been turned on, she said, "That's more than likely it! It would explain everything you've been going through!" I asked her what the long-term ramifications would be, and she said I would most likely never completely recover. I refused to accept that. I firmly believed that God had better plans for me.

The longer I stayed away from Florida, the better I felt. I slowly began to regain energy. I could walk more than a few steps without being winded, and the brain fog began to clear. After about 18 months, I was finally able to go back to work.

I was blessed with an amazing job that I loved, working as a contracts manager for the international pharmaceutical industry responsible for 28 countries. I had major clients like Pfizer, Johnson and Johnston, and Lily. I went from earning about $1600 a month to making over six figures. I also met my husband, a 6'4, good-looking nuclear engineer within a year of being there. He's an amazing man who loves children as much as I do. We now live in Georgia, have nine children at home, and are beginning a farm which will be a ministerial outreach for adults with special needs.

So, I said all that to say this. If you are going through a valley right now, having just left what you thought was the perfect mountain top, please lift your head high knowing that your heavenly Father has something even better in store if you will just trust Him. Maybe you've been hurt by those you thought would stand by your side. Forgive them, and let it go. God will make the truth known. He will make your righteousness shine like the noonday sun. Remind yourself that you are the head and not the tail. You are the righteousness of God in Christ Jesus.

People may have deserted you, but God will NEVER leave you or forsake you. With Him on your side, what can man do to you? Rise up in expectation, even if the only energy you have is to raise your hands. That's what I did! I praised Him even when I hadn't the energy to stand. I prayed and praised Him from my bed, my sofa, or my friend's sofa. Wherever I was, I reminded Satan that He was not going to win the battle. God had greater things in store for me! And He has amazing things in store for you, too!

RISE UP!

Kelley Pruett Robinson is a wife, a singer, and an actor. She is the mother of five adult children and has adopted nine children. She and her family reside in Hephzibah, Georgia.

Testimony

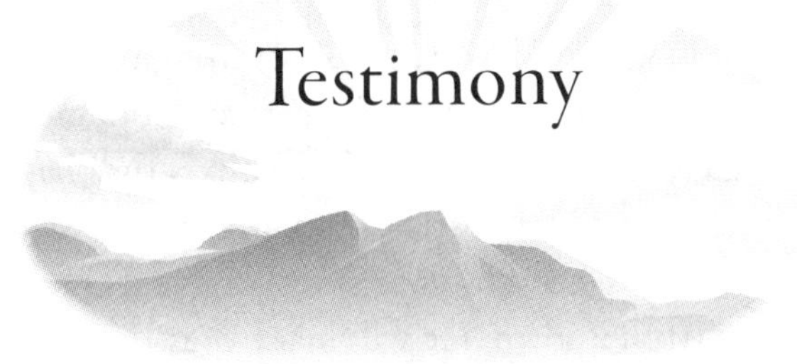

Overcoming the Pain of Grief

By Barbara J. White

OUR golden wedding anniversary was approaching. It seemed like yesterday when we were married in a little Elim Pentecostal Church in Kingston in Thames, England, in 1964. Our lives were filled with precious memories of family life and ministry to many nations.

My three children were planning a 50th anniversary celebration at a local restaurant. It had been booked when suddenly we realized it would not happen. My dear Gordon was on hospice care at home, and the responsibility of caring for him seemed overwhelming at times. The peace of God residing in my spirit held me in spite of all the emotional ups and downs of daily caregiving. The Holy Spirit showed me that Gordon would soon join the ranks of the "well done, thou good and faithful" servants. We even talked about his homegoing, but he was lovingly concerned about me.

Grief is not a subject you often talk about. It seems so remote, but you know it is awaiting—perhaps sooner rather than later. The word *grief* paints a picture of distress, sorrow, and mental and emotional suffering over loss. And the death of a loved one includes all of these. Weeping came and went each day.

I knew my purpose in God and that I should continue the ministry Gordon and I started together. I also knew to take time to adjust to my new status and not be in a hurry to go forward. It never bothered me to be called a widow. I knew from the Word of God how much He loves and cares for widows.

Just six weeks after my husband's death, I received a surprising invitation! A longtime ministry friend invited me to accompany her on a mission's trip to Mexico, and the whole trip was like medicine from heaven. When I forgot about myself and my pain, the Lord energized me to minister to others.

Widowhood brings responsibilities you never had beforehand. I quickly learned to make decisions based on the Word of God. I knew I must never retreat and especially never allow myself to go backward into self-pity and depression. I knew I had authority as a believer to stop it by saying NO and telling the enemy to take his hands off me. God gave me great grace as He promises in His Word.

I did many practical things each day. I made a to-do list every evening to help me keep focused the following day. I also took walks, phoned friends, and wrote in a journal. Six months after becoming a widow, I decided to get myself a little dog, and she is such great company and a blessing.

The wonderful ministry of the Holy Spirit is to help us and to show us things to come. I knew my future in God was so wonderful, but it wouldn't happen automatically. He expected me to make faith decisions and press through the emotional realm with His ability. When I accepted the reality of my circumstances, it placed me in the position to receive the supernatural comfort provided by the Holy Spirit. To deny my present situation would have held me in bondage.

It is faith decisions that guided me along the path of victory. The spiritual forces provided for us in God's Word and present within my spirit, drawn upon, brought healing to my pain and disappointments. Disappointment is not my destination. I am passing through life with grace and victory in the power of the Holy Spirit.

Spending time in the Word of God brought great peace and comfort to my soul, and I spent time praying in the Spirit. My healing was not mind over grief. It came about by releasing the power of God in my spirit through praying in tongues that brought about a supernatural release in my soul. It is the Spirit that gives life; to be spiritually minded is life and peace (Rom. 8:6).

Barbara J. White is cofounder of Faith Ministries International located in Corona, California, and author of *Navigating through the Pain of Grief* and *Winning Widows.*

Insomnia & Nightmares

You will sleep like a baby, safe and sound—
your rest will be sweet and secure.

Proverbs 3:24 TPT

Sweet Sleep

FATHER, thank You for peaceful sleep and for Your angels that encamp around us who fear You. You deliver us and keep us safe. The angels excel in strength, do Your word, and heed the voice of Your Word. You give Your angels charge over me, to keep me in all my ways.

I bring every thought, every imagination, and every dream into the captivity and obedience of Jesus Christ right now in Jesus' name. My mind—awake or asleep—will be clear and free from fear. I will rest without a worry and sleep soundly.

Father, thank You that even as I sleep, my heart counsels me and reveals to me Your purpose and plan. Thank You for sweet sleep, for You promised Your beloved sweet sleep. Therefore, my heart is glad, and my spirit rejoices. My body and soul rest and confidently dwell in safety. I will awake refreshed and ready for my day in Jesus' name, amen.

SCRIPTURE REFERENCES

Proverbs 3:24 Voice, CEV • Psalm 91:11 • Psalm 34:7
2 Corinthians 10:5 • Psalm 103:20 NKJV • Psalm 127:2

Overcoming Nightmares

FATHER-GOD, I know that You never sleep or slumber, but thank You for being my shield and my fortress and caring for me while I do. Holy Spirit, I ask You to help me interpret the underlying cause of these nightmares because I know that You have not given me a spirit of fear but a spirit of power, love, and a sound mind.

I choose to fix all my thoughts on You, and You will keep me in perfect peace because I trust in You. Jesus, You give me peace that the world cannot understand, and You will keep my heart and mind even as I sleep.

My deep need calls out to the deep kindness of Your love. Your waterfall of weeping sent waves of sorrow over my soul, carrying me away, cascading over me like a thundering cataract. Yet all day long Your promises of love pour over me. Through the night I sing Your songs. Thank You for commanding Your heavenly messengers to guard me and keep me safe in every way.

Before I sleep, I believe and meditate on Your Word, knowing that You, the Lord of peace, will give me peace at all times in every situation—even at night!

I will not be afraid when I go to bed, and I will sleep soundly through the night. I will be refreshed with sweet sleep. Lord, You are with me, and You protect me! I pray in Jesus' name, amen.

SCRIPTURE REFERENCES

Psalm 4:8 TLB • Isaiah 26:3 • Philippians 4:7 • Psalm 42:6-8 TPT
John 14:27 • Psalm 91:11 Voice • 2 Thessalonians 3:16 TPT
Proverbs 3:23-25 GNT, Voice, TLB

An Oasis of Peace

FATHER, I choose to focus on Your Word. You know all that my body needs, so I will never be worried about my life or about necessary sleep that my body needs. You care for the birds, and You provide their needs. I am much more valuable to You than the birds, and I know that worrying will add nothing to my life.

You are the Creator who swept into being the spangled heavens, the earth, and all their hosts in six days. I remember that on the seventh day—with the canvas of the cosmos completed—You paused from Your labor and rested. Here at the close of the day, Your presence is with me, and You will give me rest.

LORD, You are my best friend and my shepherd. You offer a resting place for me in Your luxurious love, and Your tracks take me to an oasis of peace. That's where You restore and revive my life. Father, I choose to fill my thoughts with Your words until they penetrate deep into my spirit. Then, as I unwrap Your words, they will impart true life and radiant health into the very core of my being.

You give rest to those You love, and You love me! Thank You, Father, that I will sleep like a baby, safe, and sound—my rest will be sweet and secure. In the name of Jesus. Amen

SCRIPTURE REFERENCES

Matthew 6:25-34 TPT • Genesis 2:1-3 Voice • Exodus 33:14
Psalm 23 TPT • Proverbs 4:21-22 TPT
Proverbs 3:23-25 TPT • Psalm 127:2 MSG

Praise: Surrounded with Your Glory

FATHER, I praise and worship You in spirit and in truth. You are my Shield and You surround me with Yourself.

Your glory covers me continually. Whenever and about whatever troubles me, You lift high my head. I praise You for sending me help just when I need Your presence to surround me.

So now I'll lie down and sleep like a baby—then I'll awake in safety for You surround me with Your glory!

SCRIPTURE REFERENCES

John 4:24 • Psalm 3:3-6 TPT

Testimony

Goodnight and Goodbye to Nightmares

By Kalea Ellison

I'M naturally a night owl, but combine that with stress and financial pressure, and you end up with a lot of sleepless nights. As a single girl in my mid-twenties, I would lie awake at night playing scenarios in my mind to try and come up with a solution to my financial problems. Before I knew it, I was thinking about mistakes I had made years ago, wishing I had not been foolish enough to make them. If only I had seen the traps of the enemy *before* I walked into them.

Next thing I knew, I was having flashbacks to my childhood traumatic experiences. But by that time, it was too late. I had already given my mind free reign, and there was no stopping that train. I would try replacing those thoughts with "happy thoughts," but it wasn't enough. I was miserable. I would lie down to go to sleep, and finally, after about three to five hours, I would become so mentally exhausted that I would fall asleep.

Then came the nightmares. I would dream that I was having fun with friends, jumping on a trampoline, but somehow, I managed to jump too high. I'd climb higher and higher until I knew that if I began to fall, I would likely die once I met the ground. Being from Hawaii, I often had fun surfing dreams. But on those stressful nights, I would dream of swimming in the ocean, enjoying myself only to encounter trouble. I'd dive down to the ocean floor to pick up a seashell, and I would take too long to find the surface again. I'd swim my hardest and fastest, but the surface only got farther away.

I'd also dream that I was asleep in my bed when my friends and family came to visit. As they all began to arrive, I would try to wake up, but my eyes wouldn't open all the way. My friends and family thought I was asleep, so they would all leave, assuming I didn't care enough to get out of bed for them. I'd cry so hard in my dream that I'd wake up with tears in my eyes.

One day in Bible school, my instructor told a story about how he was extremely stressed at certain point in his life, but he got ahold of Philippians 4:8. Naturally, this intrigued me. He told us how he would quote this scripture at night, but he would put himself in it. He would say "I *refuse* to think on anything that's not true, noble, just, pure, lovely, of good report, virtuous or praiseworthy!" And he would repeat this any time he got worried. I decided to give it a try. I mean, it couldn't hurt, right? I was already lying in bed awake for five hours a night. I might as well spend it quoting the Scriptures.

That night, as I laid down to sleep, the stressful thoughts began to flood my mind as usual, so I quoted Philippians 4:8 the way my instructor had. The thoughts subsided! for about 15 seconds. So, I quoted it again. The thoughts subsided for about 15 seconds. I repeated this cycle about 55-60 times until I finally fell asleep. I did this every night for approximately one week. I would imagine each thought going through a quality control conveyor belt in my mind. Is that thought true? Is it noble? Is it just? And so on.

If the thought couldn't pass the full Philippians 4:8 test, I moved on. At the end of that week, I began to notice that I wasn't having to quote the scripture 55-60 times a night. It was more like 45-50. As the weeks went on, I stayed faithful to quoting Philippians 4:8. Eventually, I was only quoting the scripture once, right as I laid down to sleep. I'd have a clear head to be able to talk to the Holy Spirit until I fell asleep peacefully.

I figured out what I'd been doing wrong all that time: 1) I was letting my mind run away with me, unchecked, for too long before I attempted to counteract it. 2) I was trying to counteract thoughts with thoughts. When the devil picks a fight with you, don't fight fair! Just "thinking happy thoughts" will not get the job done. You've got to bring a bigger, stronger weapon to the fight: your WORDS. You've got to REFUSE to think on anything that's not true, noble, just, pure, lovely, of good report, virtuous, or praiseworthy! God helped me, and He will help you too!

Kalea Ellison is a writer and musician who can also be found on the sets of indie films in her spare time. She's authored a children's book titled *Sometimes I... Dream* to help children not be fearful when falling asleep. Kalea resides in Broken Arrow, Oklahoma.

Panic Attacks & PTSD

Dear friend, guard Clear Thinking and
Common Sense with your life; don't for a minute
lose sight of them. They'll keep your soul alive
and well, they'll keep you fit and attractive. You'll
travel safely, you'll neither tire nor trip. You'll take
afternoon naps without a worry, you'll enjoy
a ***good night's sleep. No need to panic***
over alarms or surprises, or predictions
that doomsday's *just around the corner,*
Because God will be right there with you;
he'll keep you safe and sound.

Proverbs 3:21-16 MSG

Spare Me from the Harm of My Past

Meditation

Since the beginning of time as we know it, Lucifer has plotted and planned to turn mankind against God. I thank God for the advances of the medical profession. Scientists continue trying to find a pill that will cure those with "mental disorders." I thank God for counselors and those who base their therapy on love because God *is* Love!

Jesus came to bring us life—He healed the sick, caused the lame to walk, opened blind eyes, and raised the dead. "Jesus of Nazareth was anointed by God with the Holy Spirit and with great power. He did wonderful things for others and divinely healed all who were under the tyranny of the devil for God anointed him."[37]

Is there anything too hard for our God?[38] Are mental disorders too hard for our God? Are panic attacks and post-traumatic stress disorder (PTSD) too hard for God? NO! As you apply the following prayer therapy, the Holy Spirit will work with you and your mind will be renewed. You will learn to love others as you love yourself, and your walking-about-life and your sleeping-life will adjust to a new and living way! The Holy Spirit is your constant companion and with your own ears you will hear Him say, "This is the way you should go, whether to the right or to the left." [39]

Let me add that "blunting ourselves with drugs is not the answer to overwhelming emotions. Intense emotions should be welcomed. Emotions are the vital signs of life. We need and should want them to be strong. We also need our brains and minds to be functioning at

---

37 Acts 10:38 TPT

38 Genesis 18:14 NLT

39 Isaiah 30:20-22 NLT

their best, free of toxic drugs. That allows us to use our intelligence and understanding to the fullest. Thinking clearly is one of the hallmarks of taking charge of oneself instead of caving into helplessness."[40]

Prayer

Father-God, I need understanding about these flashbacks and emotions that overwhelm me. Holy Spirit, I ask You to help me pray when I do not know what to pray. I've poured out my life before You, and in spite of these feelings of dread, guilt, and fear, I know that You are always here for me. So now I ask You to teach me more of Your holy decrees. Open up my understanding to the ways of Your wisdom, and I will meditate deeply on Your splendor and Your wonders.

My life's strength melts away with grief and sadness. Come strengthen me and encourage me with Your words, my Lord and my God. You have gone into my future to prepare the way, and in kindness You follow behind me to spare me from the harm of my past. With Your hand of love upon my life, You impart a blessing to me. This is just too wonderful and incomprehensible!

Your understanding of me brings me wonder and strength. You see and You know the trauma of the past. Your Spirit was with me, and I did not run and hide from Your face. When I am oppressed, I come to You as a shelter in the time of trouble. You are a perfect hiding place. I know Your mercy, and I am putting my trust in You, for I can count on You for help no matter what.

Lord, You will never—no never—neglect anyone who comes to You. Thank You for hearing my prayer. In the name of Jesus, amen.

Scriptures References

Psalm 119:26-28 TPT • Psalm 139:5-7 TPT • Psalm 9:9-11 TPT

---

40 Breggin, Peter R. "Empathic Therapy®: Psychiatric Drug Facts." *Peter Breggin, MD: Psychiatric Drug Facts,* breggin.com/empathic-therapy/.

When Affliction Strikes

LORD, may I never forget the promises You have made to me, for they are my hope and confidence. In all of my affliction, even here in the night, I find great comfort in Your promises for they have kept me alive. No matter how bitterly the voices mock me, I refuse to budge from Your precepts. Rescue me! Pull me into victory and breakthrough. You are my high fortress, where I'm kept safe. You are to me a stronghold of salvation. When You deliver me out of this peril, it will bring glory to Your name.

As You guide me forth, I'll be kept safe from the hidden snares of the enemy—the secret traps that lie before me—for You have become my rock of strength. I despise these deceptive illusions, all this pretense and nonsense, for I worship only You. In mercy You have seen my troubles and cared for me; even during this crisis in my soul I choose to be radiant with joy, filled with praise for Your love and mercy.

I'm desperate, Lord! I throw myself upon You, for You alone are my God! Let my shame and disgrace be replaced by Your favor once again. Lord, Your name is blessed and lifted high! Thank You for Your marvelous miracle of mercy that protects me when I feel overwhelmed by emotional stress.

SCRIPTURE REFERENCES

Psalm 119:49-51 TPT • Psalm 31 TPT

Victory over Post-Traumatic Stress Disorder (PTSD)

FATHER-GOD, with the help of the Holy Spirit, I choose to bring my thoughts, this feeling of guilt, the nightmares, the bad memories, and all that I am to You. Give me mercy from Your fountain of forgiveness.

Even in my darkness moments You were there; when I violated my own conscience, You grieved with me. When I was abused and violated, or witnessed and encountered the horrific, You knew. The trauma of all that I've experienced continues to hang on, but I know that Jesus came to set the captives free.

I know Your abundant love is enough to wash away my guilt, and because Your compassion is so great, You take away this shameful guilt of sin. I know Your abundant love is enough to remove the sting and terror of stubborn memories. I surrender to You, Father, and today I choose to stand up to the devil and resist him, and he will turn and run away from me.

I move my heart closer and closer to You, and You will come even closer to me. I choose to cleanse my mind of the trauma of the past and keep my heart pure, and I choose to replace my doubting with the Word of God.

Jesus, You came to give me life—even abundant life—and I walk in the freedom of the Holy Spirit who is my constant Companion.

SCRIPTURE REFERENCES

Psalm 51:1 TPT • James 4:7-8 TPT • John 10:10

A Life Abundant and Free

JESUS, I believe that You are the Way, the Truth, and the Life, and You came to give me Life—abundant life. I know that I am here for such a time as this, and I am valuable to You.

Father, teach me to walk victoriously in my new-found freedom. You rescued me completely from the tyrannical rule of darkness, and You translated me into the kingdom realm of Your beloved Son. I thank You that I am victorious over PTSD because in the Son all my sins are canceled, and I have the release of redemption through His very blood. With Your sacred blood, You thoroughly cleanse my conscience of things I may have done that are wrong and the memory of wrong things others have done to me. For by the power of the eternal Spirit, Jesus offered Himself to God as the perfect Sacrifice that now frees me from my dead works to worship and serve You, the living God, my Father!

I no longer have to live under a low-lying black cloud. Now no condemnation awaits those who are living in Jesus the Anointed, the Liberating King! The case is closed! There remains no accusing voice of condemnation against those who are joined in life-union with Jesus!

Father, I will stop dwelling on the past and not even remember these former things! I won't keep going over old history. I'm leaving my old life behind, putting everything on the line for this mission. I am sprinting toward the only goal that counts: to cross the line, to win the prize, and to hear Your call to resurrection life found exclusively in Jesus the Anointed. I don't depend on my own strength to accomplish this. I fasten my heart to the future. The old is gone—and see—a new life has begun!

SCRIPTURE REFERENCES

John 14:6 • Colossians 1:14 TPT • Hebrews 9:14 TPT • Romans 8:1 MSG, Voice, TPT • Philippians 3:13-14 Voice, TPT
Isaiah 43:18-19 TPT, MSG • 2 Corinthians 5:17 Voice

My Supernatural Helper

FATHER-GOD, thank You for sending the Comforter, who is my Counselor, Helper, Intercessor, Advocate, Strengthener, and Standby, the Holy Spirit. My supernatural Helper will teach me all things.

I receive the peace that You left with me. I choose Your peace, and by Your grace I purpose not to let my heart be troubled, neither let it be afraid. I will no longer allow myself to be agitated and disturbed. I will not permit myself to be fearful, intimidated, cowardly, unsettled, or panicked.

I submit to the Spirit of Truth who has come to guide me in all truth. He does not speak His own words to me, but He speaks what He hears, revealing to me the things to come and bringing glory to You. He will take me by the hand and guide me, and He will unveil the reality of every truth within me.

Jesus, You have told me these things so that I will be whole and at peace. In this world, I am plagued with times of trouble, but I need not fear for You have triumphed over this corrupt world order.

Father-God, I know that Your peace (a peace that is beyond any and all of our human understanding) will stand watch over my heart and mind in Jesus, the Anointed One. Your peace keeps my thoughts and heart quiet and at rest. Jesus Christ displaces worry at the center of my life!

SCRIPTURE REFERENCES

John 14:26-27 AMPC • John 16:13-15, 33 Voice, MSG, TPT
Philippians 4:7 Voice, MSG, TLB

Praise Silences Panic Attacks and PTSD

FATHER-GOD, there is no one like You! Were You not here, who would protect me from panic attacks and PTSD? If You don't stand to defend me, who will? I have no one but You!

I would have died so many times if You had not been there for me. When I screamed out, "Lord, I'm doomed!" Your fiery love was stirred, and You raced to my rescue. Whenever my busy thoughts were out of control, the soothing comfort of Your presence calmed me down and overwhelmed me with delight.

Praise the name of the Lord, for all who are oppressed may come to You as a shelter in the time of trouble. You are a perfect hiding place. I know Your mercy, and I will continue trusting You for I can count on You for help no matter what.

O Lord, You will never, no never, neglect me when I come to You. I am singing out my praises to my God who lives and rules within Zion. I purpose to tell the world about all the miracles You have done for me!

SCRIPTURE REFERENCES

Psalm 94:16-19 TPT • Psalm 9:9-11 TPT

Praise: Radiant with Joy

FATHER, I overflow with triumphant joy in our relationship, living in harmony with You—all because of Jesus Christ! You are upholding me with Your victorious right hand, and I make it my primary goal to know You more intimately.

You have made me glad, and I rejoice here in Your presence. I am laughing and radiant with joy! Thank You for sending angels with special orders to protect me wherever I go, defending me from all harm.

SCRIPTURE REFERENCES

Psalm 68:2-4 TPT • Psalm 91:11 TPT

Testimony

Triumph over Excruciating Pain and Traumatic Stress

By Dr. John Turner, D.C.

It was in 2003 my own journey with traumatic stress began, I had no idea of how my life would be changed in the next few years and how God would use my own traumatic stress to be a blessing to thousands of people all over the world who suffer from anxiety, panic attacks, depression, and PTSD.

I started my first clinical practice in 1986, which I quickly outgrew and moved to larger building in Roswell, Georgia. It was an exciting time, and God had given me a vision for healing and restoring hurting people who I have held deep in my heart all these years.

One evening while leaving my office, I was involved in a serious automobile accident. I was hit by a drunk driver at a speed of 80 miles an hour right in front of my office building. I suffered a broken back that required emergency surgery and was left with unrelenting, unbearable pain in my back and legs that continued for over a year. I was unable to return to work for many months, and when I did return, my hours were very limited.

I was a competitive swimmer and triathlete before the accident. It was devastating to me to then be physically debilitated and dependent on drugs. I watched as my once-thriving practice began to shrivel. Little did I know, the stress of the emotional and physical trauma following the accident was just beginning.

As life would have it, I experienced a freak accident the very next year that severed my Achilles tendon. This injury was more crippling than the previous one, resulting in a long-term systemic infection and excruciating chronic pain. Again, I found myself having one surgery after another. Unfortunately, this surgery brought such a serious infection that I had to go against everything I believed in, including taking massive doses of long-term IV antibiotics and more pain pills.

I have to admit that there were many days that I couldn't find God in all the pain. But as faithful as He is, He began to guide and direct my recovery. I began to read, pray, and dig deep into neurological research to discover things I had never considered before in my professional career as a chiropractor. It is through God's divine guidance and searching for my personal recovery that God began to reveal insights to me regarding how trauma effects the brain and nervous system and scientific ways to resolve it working with the limbic system.

In my research, I found confirmation in the Center for Disease (CDC) Ace study (www.cdc.gov./ace). It's the largest healthcare study ever completed, demonstrating how trauma in one's life, especially in early childhood, can cause health care problems in the future. This is a direct result of the brain's limbic system stuck in fight or flight mode.

We all have a filter in our brains called the limbic system, better known as the "fight or flight." This is a survival mechanism in the brain that God designed to protect us from harm. Our brain reacts the same in response to physical or emotional pain by releasing the stress chemicals, adrenaline, and cortisol to take quick action when we are in an unsafe situation. Unfortunately, these unresolved stresses over a period of time lead to anxiety, depression, and a host of other physical and mental illness according to the CDC Ace study.

We are instructed as believers to cast our cares on the Lord. What God taught me was that out of tragedy comes greatness. Just as Christ went through the darkest valley and even felt forsaken in His greatest time of pain, we know God has a higher purpose we as humans are not always able to understand.

It's often times difficult to see the light when you are living in the shadows of despair and depression that accompany PTSD or deep emotional or physical trauma. It is my prayer that my story will offer some light and encouragement to those of you suffering and wondering, *Where is God in all of this?* Be still and know that He is there.

I was broken emotionally and physically. God was able to use the deep physical and emotional trauma I suffered to help others. In the process, God gave me insights on how to help people resolve emotional and physical stress.

I have been free from both pain and the depression that comes with post-traumatic stress since 2006. I now teach doctors all over the world how to help resolve emotional traumas and relieve physical pain by working with the limbic system.

In the years since, I have had the opportunity to work with thousands of clients who have suffered some of the most horrendous tragedies one can imagine. It is possible to find your way out of emotional despair. God's will is for us to walk in the Spirit, to rejoice, pray, and give thanks in all things.

When you find yourself in the darkest hour, remember this could be part of your future success story. Ask God to use you and mold you so that you may be able to lift up and encourage others.

I pray that your recovery will be quick and lead you to the freedom from your own physical challenges and emotional shocks and traumas and that shortly you will be able to see the divine purpose for your own healing that God has in store for you.

Dr. John Turner, D.C., founder and creator of QNRT®, Pinnacle Health Services, a brain-based wellness center, located in Roswell, Georgia.

Testimony

From Daily Panic Attacks to Complete and Lasting Freedom

By Victoria Bowling

SEVERAL years ago, I found myself in the emergency room with alarming symptoms. I thought I was having a heart attack or a stroke! I had chest pains. I could not breathe, and half of my body went numb. After a battery of testing, the emergency room doctor told me I was suffering from panic disorder. My doctor confirmed his diagnosis but also informed me that I was clinically depressed. She prescribed a couple of different medications for me.

The months leading up to this dramatic climax were filled with one stressful event after another. I barely had time to catch my breath in between the seemingly never-ending stream of chaos and trauma. Eventually, it took a huge toll on me.

There were major issues with our three teenage sons. It seemed like an onslaught straight out of hell had been unleashed against them. There were the pressures of the ministry. At the time, I owned a business and some of my employees were causing some serious problems. To top it off, I discovered that someone had spread a bunch of untruths about me to most of my family and friends.

As the stress piled up upon me like a heavy weight, my body reacted with panic attacks. I began to experience two to three full-blown anxiety attacks every day. I would have to stop whatever I was doing, lie on the floor, and wait for my body to stop shaking uncontrollably as wave after wave of terror washed over me. It was sheer hell.

I was surprised to be diagnosed with depression. I am not sure why since I went to bed crying every night and woke up crying every morning for six months straight because of the unbearable grief I was enduring, mostly over the attacks on my sons. Looking back, it made sense. The first part of Proverbs 12:25 says, "Anxiety in the heart of a man causes depression." That was certainly the case with me!

The medication gave me instant relief. It provided me with a "pause" so I could get my footing. I was angry, embarrassed, and confused. How in the world could I have ended up this way? The panic attacks lessened in intensity, and my tears dried a little. But I did not want to depend on medication for stability. Thankfully, I knew that my answer was the Word of God. I have always been a person who searches the Scriptures for promises to change the circumstances in my life. I focused on scriptures about healing and peace, sought the Lord, and prayed in tongues.

One day a friend called me and said, "Victoria, I have a word from God for you!" I was all ears. I was desperate. "Every time you feel that panic start to come on you, open up your mouth and say, 'I am righteous by the blood of Jesus!'" *Wait a minute!* I thought. *Is that it? I have been suffering miserably for months and that is all I need to do?* I was a little offended at first. I mean, there I was, a Bible school graduate serving in full-time ministry for over two decades with my husband. I already know that I am righteous by the blood of Jesus! It seemed way too simple.

It was simple. And it worked! I began to say it out loud every time I felt the panic coming. I did not just say it. I *thought* about it. I pictured myself inside of Jesus, and Jesus inside of me. I envisioned His blood washing over me and making me righteous. Little by little, the anxiety started to dissipate. I was thrilled! I kept meditating on it and speaking it.

Soon after, my husband found scriptures in the Bible that gave me some clear insight as to *why* it worked. Isaiah 54:14, "In righteousness you shall be established; You shall be far from oppression, for you shall not fear; And from terror, for it shall not come near you" (NKJV). Isaiah 32:17 says, "The work of righteousness will be peace, And the effect of righteousness, quietness and assurance forever" (NKJV).

The lightbulb went on, and I saw the connection between the righteousness of God working in us and walking in true peace. I literally immersed myself in scriptures about my righteousness in Christ Jesus until every bit of anxiety was eradicated from my life. The depression soon followed! I was able to wean off my meds, and I have been free ever since!

Victoria Bowling and her husband, Mark, are founders of Global Impact Ministries International, a ministry dedicated to taking the gospel of Jesus Christ to the unreached people of the world. They make their home in Broken Arrow, Oklahoma.

Suicide

I call heaven and earth as witnesses today against you, that I have set before you life and death, blessing and cursing; therefore ***choose life,*** *that both you and your descendants may live.*

Deuteronomy 30:19 NKJV

Choosing Life

LORD, reach down from heaven, all the way from the sky to the sea, and reach down into my darkness to rescue me! Thoughts of despair hound me day and night, and I'm turning toward the mercy seat as I lift my hands in surrendered prayer. Take me out of my calamity and chaos and draw me to Yourself. Take me from the depths of my despair. The thoughts of suicide are overwhelming, and I'm asking You to deliver me.

I humble myself before You and ask You to bring heaven's deliverance, and all at once, turn on a floodlight for me! You are the revelations-light in my darkness and in Your brightness, I can see the path ahead. With You as my strength I can take captive every thought of suicide.

I choose life. I shall live and not die in the name of Jesus and trust You for a brighter day.

SCRIPTURE REFERENCES

Psalm 28:1-2 TPT • Psalm 18:15-17, 27-29 TPT

The Art of Training My Mind

Lord, today I choose to begin training my mind and renouncing thoughts of death for a total reformation of how I think. I surrender myself to You to be Your sacred, living sacrifice and live in holiness, experiencing all that delights Your heart.

Lord, You know everything there is to know about me. You perceive every movement of my heart and soul, and You understand my every thought before it even enters my mind. You are so intimately aware of my every thought, and You read my heart like an open book. You know all the words I'm about to speak before I even start a sentence. You know every step I will take before my journey even begins. You have gone into my future to prepare the way, and in kindness You follow behind me to spare me from the harm of my past. With Your hand of love upon my life, You impart a blessing to me.

Today, I choose to fix my heart on Your promises, and I will be secure, feasting on Your faithfulness. God, You are my utmost delight and the pleasure of my life, and You will provide for me what I desire the most. I choose to give You the right to direct my life, and as I trust You along the way, I'll find that You pulled it off perfectly! In Jesus' name I pray, amen.

SCRIPTURE REFERENCES

Romans 8:1 • Psalm 139:1-5 TPT • Psalm 36:3-6 TPT

Divine Strength

FATHER, forgive me. I have allowed my thoughts to take me to a dark place, and I've never considered renewing my mind or taking control of my thoughts. It never occurred to me that I could align my thoughts with Yours, but Your Word makes it clear that we do not have to think every thought that comes into our minds (2 Cor. 10:4-5).

Once I was blind, but now I can see. Thank You for bringing sight to my blind eyes, and now I can see the wrong perceptions that were contrary to Your Word. The weapons of the war we all fight are not of this world but are powered by You and effective at tearing down the strongholds erected against Your truth. I demolish arguments and ideas, every high-and-mighty philosophy that pits itself against the knowledge of the one true God. I take prisoners of every thought, every emotion, subduing them into obedience to the Anointed One.

Right now, I submit my perceptions, my thoughts, and my emotions to You to be cleansed by the washing of water by the Word. You have not given me a spirit of fear but a spirit of love, power, and a sound mind.

I choose to surrender all that I am to You, and I will be saved from the lies that held me captive.

I exchange my weaknesses for Your strengths in every area of life. Your grace is sufficient for me! Your power is made perfect in my weakness. Because of YOU, I can be my strongest when I feel weakest.

I wait for Yahweh's grace, and I experience divine strength. I rise up on soaring wings and fly like an eagle. I will run my race without growing weary and walk through life without giving up.

I walk out of darkness into the light of Your Word, for the law of the Spirit of life has liberated me from the law of sin and death.

SCRIPTURE REFERENCES

Romans 8:1-2 • John 9:1-7 • Ephesians 5:26-27 • 2 Timothy 1:7
2 Corinthians 12:8 TPT • Isaiah 40:31 TPT • Romans 12:1-2

Amazing Grace

FATHER, I live in a world of deception and darkness. Yet, You made me in Your image—spirit, soul, and body. I am delivered from the power of deception, and so I discard every form of dishonesty and lying so that I will be known as one who always speaks the truth. No longer will I allow the passion of my emotions to lead me to sin! Anger (self-anger) will no longer control me and be fuel for revenge, not for even a day. I no longer believe the slanderous accuser, the devil. I am free from his manipulation.

It is only through Your wonderful, amazing grace that I believed in You. Nothing I did could ever have earned so wonderful a salvation, for it is the gracious gift from You that brought me to Christ!

I walk by faith and not by sight. You have removed my guilt from me the same way a loving father feels toward his children, and that's but a sample of Your tender feelings toward me, Your beloved child, who now lives in awe of You.

You know all about me—inside and out—and You are mindful that I am made from dust. I am Yours, and You are mine. It is Christ in me, the hope of glory!

Thank You for giving me the Spirit of Truth who guards me from deception. Thank You for rescuing my soul from death's fear and drying my eyes of many tears. You keep my feet firmly on the path You have chosen for me, and You strengthen me so that I may please You, my life before You in Your life-giving light!

SCRIPTURE REFERENCES

Genesis 1:26 • Ephesians 2:8-9 TPT • Ephesians 4:25-27 TPT
Psalm 103:12-14 TPT • Psalm 116:18-19 TPT

Crucified with Christ

Meditation

"I have been crucified with Christ; it is no longer I who live, but Christ lives in me; and the life which I now live in the flesh I live by faith in the Son of God, who loved me and gave Himself for me" (Galatians 2:20 NKJV).

Prayer

FATHER, I know Your ears are open to my prayers, and I thank You for hearing my prayer and answering me. I am worn out by my worries and crushed by oppression. I am gripped by fear and trembling. Oh, that I had wings like a dove! I would fly away and be at rest. Yes, I would wander far away; I would lodge in the wilderness. I would hasten to escape and to find a shelter from the stormy wind and tempest.

I am calling upon You, my God, to rescue me. You redeem my life in peace from the battle of hopelessness that is against me. I cast my burden on You, Lord, releasing the weight of it, and You sustain me. You will never allow the consistently righteous to be moved—made to slip, fall, or fail.

Hopelessness lies in wait for me to swallow me up or trample me all day long. Whenever I am afraid, I will have confidence in and put my trust and reliance in You. By Your help, God, I will praise Your Word. On You I lean, rely, and confidently put my trust. I will not fear!

You know my every sleepless night. Each tear and heartache is answered with Your promise. I am thanking You with all my heart. You pulled me from the brink of death, my feet from the cliff edge of doom. Now I stroll at leisure with You in the sunlit fields of life.

What, what would have become of me, Lord, had I not believed that I would see Your goodness in the land of the living! I wait and hope for and expect You. I am brave and of good courage, and I let my heart be stout and enduring. Yes, I wait for and hope for and expect You.

Father, I give You all my worries and cares, for You are always thinking about me and watching everything that concerns me. I am well-balanced and careful—vigilant, watching out for attacks from Satan, my great enemy. By Your grace I am standing firm, trusting You, and I remember that other Christians all around the world are going through these sufferings too. You, God, are full of kindness through Christ and will give me Your eternal glory.

In the name of Jesus, I am an overcomer by the blood of the Lamb and by the word of my testimony. Amen.

SCRIPTURE REFERENCES

Hebrews 4:16 • Psalm 56:5,8 MSG • Psalm 55:1-5 GNT • Psalm 56:13 MSG
Psalm 27:13,14 AMPC • Psalm 55:6-8 AMPC • 1 Peter 5:7-9 AMPC, TLB
Psalm 55:16,18,22 AMPC • Revelation 12:11 • Psalm 56:2-4 AMPC

Praise: Living to Praise

FATHER, You have given me the choice between life and death. Now with heaven and earth as my witnesses, I choose life that I and my descendants might live! You knew me before You formed me in my mother's womb, and before I was born You set me apart and appointed me to live on earth for such a time as this.

You are my Creator, and You knit me together in my mother's womb. You made me so wonderfully complex! I am Your marvelous workmanship! With Your help I will take full advantage of every day as I spend my life for Your purposes, and I choose not to live foolishly so I will have discernment to fully understand Your will and purpose for my life here on earth. You have given me a spirit of power, love, and a sound mind. Thank You, Father-God, for your tender love and faithful care of me!

SCRIPTURE REFERENCES

Deuteronomy 30:19 NLT • Jeremiah 1:5 NLT
Psalm 139:13-14 NLT • Ephesians 5:15-16 TPT

Testimony

'I Tried to End My Life Many Times until God Healed, Restored, and Set Me Free'

By Kylie Oaks Gatewood

NOT long ago I celebrated my 40th birthday, which was a big deal because there was a time when I didn't know if I'd live past my 20s. As a 20-year-old, my life looked pretty good on the surface. I didn't party, drink, or do any of the things that preachers' kids notoriously do. I even attended RHEMA Bible Training Center, but gradually, things changed for the worse. At the bottom of it all was an issue I had covered up for over 15 years. A man close to my family secretly molested me repeatedly for three years when I was six years old. He threatened to kill me or anyone I told, so as a child, I lived in constant fear.

As I entered my early 20s, pain, agony, anxiety, and unforgiveness continued to build up within me. I knew God's Word and knew what I should be doing to defeat the enemy's attacks, but I wasn't doing it. It reached the point where my own mind tormented me, so I started drinking to quiet the thoughts. Eventually, I became a hard-core drinker, but the more I drank the more depressed I became. I tried to lay off the alcohol but became more depressed. It was a no-win situation. My life was a total mess!

One day, I fully bought into the enemy's lies: *No one cares about you anyway. No one would care if you weren't here. Why don't you just kill yourself?* This led to my first suicide attempt. I tried to overdose on a bottle of pills, but to my disappointment, somebody found me. I woke up in the ER mad. I was diagnosed with borderline personality disorder and started medications and therapy. Experts told me I would deal with this issue for the rest of my life. I let the devil bombard my mind with lies, which ultimately led to suicide attempt number two. That time, I tried to cut my wrists.

I was at the bottom of the bottom. I lost my job, lived in a car, and was completely homeless. This was definitely *not* God's plan. Still, over and over, I listened to the devil's lies. After multiple suicide attempts, doctors locked me up in the worst place imaginable—a state mental facility.

Finally, I got tired of living a defeated life, although it took me a long time to get there. I was determined to change but didn't know how. I still had no desire whatsoever to read the Bible. It was a struggle. Ultimately, I *made* myself get into God's Word, and I am living proof it works!

When I took God at His Word, I went from being suicidal and living in my car to where I am now—happily married with two beautiful daughters, a nice house, and a wonderful life. How? I chose to take authority over my soul. I'm not bragging on myself; I'm bragging on God!

If you're looking for some magic button you can push to change your life, you won't find it. What God will give you are doable steps to apply God's Word to your life so you can live victoriously!

One primary way I got through my situation was by recognizing the wiles (fiery darts) of the devil are actually thoughts, ideas, and suggestions he brings to our minds. Over and over, I read Ephesians 6:10-16, which tells us to be strong in the Lord and in the power of His might. It taught me who my enemy was and how to shut him up.

Think about the lies the devil tells you: *That person doesn't love you. You're unlovable. You're not worth anything. What good are you doing anybody? You're damaged goods.*

These fiery darts stick in your soul until you define yourself his way. But Ephesians 6 says to take the shield of faith and quench *all* the fiery darts of the devil, so crazy thoughts don't affect your life. You do this through your words!

This is the answer to everything because everything starts with a thought. Thoughts are categorized into two groups: life and death. Thoughts are not always extreme like *kill yourself,* but deadly thoughts are anything that's anti-God, anti-Christ, or anti-life. This is how I got free! And it's so practical anyone can do it!

Back then, I could not trust myself to think. I had to get down to the raw nitty-gritty and inventory every thought. *I had to think about what I was thinking about.* I couldn't let my mind wander. I took every thought into captivity and judged which pile it went into—life or death.

If the thought came to me, *No one loves you,* I would analyze that thought: Okay, that is not a life thought, so it went into the pile of death thoughts. Then I would put my hand on my forehead and confess out loud, "That is not my thought. I do not accept it. I only think thoughts of life. I do not think thoughts of death. I plead the blood of Jesus over my mind. I have the mind of Christ." A thought might come like, *I need to use the washroom.* I would judge it as good and needful.

This may sound elementary. *But it's the key to your victory! If you do this, I promise you will get free.*

At first, I did this upwards of 200 times a day. No joke! When I got stronger, I inserted scripture. I went from speaking these things to myself 200 times a day to 150, then 100, then 25, then fewer. Finally, one day I realized I had not thought about dying one single time! I became the master of my mind, and you must do the same!

One more extremely important key to walking free is FORGIVENESS. *You won't be free without forgiving.* Forgiveness is not always cute or pretty, but Jesus commands us to do. That means we *can* do it!

Unforgiveness doesn't hurt the other person, but it's a cancer to you. It gives power to the person who wronged you. In my own life, I could not stop my molester from taking my innocence as a little girl, but it was up to me whether I would allow him to control me as an adult woman. *Forgiveness is an act of faith—not how you feel.* You must choose to control your thoughts, obey God's Word, and forgive.

I tried to end my life many times until God healed, restored, and set me free! He also wants to set you free!

More people have died and shed blood over the Bible than any other book in history. Why? *Because freedom lives in this book.* And I promise you with a 100-percent guarantee that if you do the Word, you'll get the results of the Word!

Kylie Oaks Gatewood is the author of *Winning the Mind Battle* that shares her complete testimony. She has a master's degree in Christian counseling and is the granddaughter of well-known Bible teacher and author Billye Brim.

The Real You

You even formed every bone in my body when you created me in the secret place, carefully, skillfully you shaped me from nothing to something. ***You saw who you created me to be before I became me!*** *Before I'd ever seen the light of day, the number of days you planned for me were already recorded in your book. Every single moment you are thinking of me! How precious and wonderful to consider that you cherish me constantly in your every thought! O God, your desires toward me are more than the grains of sand on every shore!*

Psalm 139:15-18 TPT

Becoming Your True Child-of-God Self

Meditation

Writing out of my own experience, I can say once again that it's all been by the grace of God. He turned my storms of depression and anxiety into chariots of victory! And He will do the same for you.

Not long ago, I heard a successful psychiatrist make a statement. He said depression and anxiety as well as mental, emotional, and psychological disorders are all the result of failures in love. I understand this. As I've said before, at one time appearances were more important to my parents than relationships. So, I passed that down to my children. As I grew in the grace and knowledge of Jesus Christ, I learned to "give thanks to Father God for every person he brings into my life, and out of reverence for Christ be supportive of others in love."[41]

"Depression and anxiety might, in one way, be the sanest reaction you have. It's a signal, saying—you shouldn't have to live this way, and if you aren't helped to find a better path, you will be missing out on so much that is best about being human."[42] The good news is that we are created in God's image—we are God's children recreated in Christ Jesus!

God wired us to love and be loved. When we override the default setting of love, we separate ourselves from God who is Love. We allow the carnal mind to form thought patterns, and everything that happens to us is stored there. These mindsets can be changed through the renewing of your mind.

---

41 Ephesians 5:10-21 TPT

42 *Lost Connections*, Johann Hari, pg. 258

"When we are born, we come into this world of darkness. A world filled with suffering. Let's be clear, the light permeates all darkness, but the darkness does not yet perceive it and so languishes in suffering, conflict, fear and worry. Our objective is to learn to see light in the darkness and so rise above fear and suffering."[43]

God thought of you before the foundation of the world, and He prepared the journey you would walk. He sent Jesus to rescue you completely from the tyrannical rules of darkness and translate you into the kingdom realm of his beloved Son.[44]

Today, could be the beginning of living life as "the real you!" It may take time and effort, but God has given you a spirit of power, love, and a sound mind. Perfect love drives fear out of doors—drives it away! You will draw to yourself that which you think on the most! Fear can actually attract the very thing you fear!

"When we think, feel, and choose, our minds process the incoming knowledge and change the wiring of our brains. So if we mindfully tune in to our ability to think, feel, and choose by paying attention to our thoughts, we can understand our Perfect You, the very core of who we are—our blueprint for identity!"[45]

Before you begin praying again, I leave you with one of my favorite passages in Scripture:

"I'm not saying that I have this all together, that I have it made. But I am well on my way, reaching out for Christ, who has so wondrously reached out for me. Friends, don't get me wrong: By no means do I count myself an expert in all of this, but I've got my eye on the goal, where God is beckoning us onward—to Jesus. I'm off and running, and I'm not turning back" (Phil. 3:12-14 MSG).

---

43 *The Way of Love,* Ted Dekker, pg. 62

44 Colossians 1:13 TPT

45 *The Perfect You,* Dr. Caroline Leaf, pg. 42

So let's keep focused on that goal, those of us who want everything God has for us. If any of you have something else in mind, something less than total commitment, God will clear your blurred vision—you'll see it yet! Now that we're on the right track, let's stay on it.[46]

Prayer

Father, once I was blind but now for the first time, I can see. I choose Jesus, the light of the world, and I am now experiencing the life-giving light! I can see the Life-Light that is the real thing. I believe that You are who You claim to be and that You will do what You said. You are making me to be my true self, my child-of-God self.

The Word became flesh, and He lives among us and in us. I have seen the glory with my own eyes, the one-of-a-kind glory, like Father, like Son. You are generous inside and out, true from start to finish.

Thank You, Father-God! In Jesus' name I pray, amen.

SCRIPTURE REFERENCES

John 9:25 TPT • John 1:13-14 MSG • John 8:12 TPT

46 Philippians 3:12-16 MSG

Living by Faith

FATHER, I'm rejoicing! My old identity has been co-crucified with Messiah and no longer lives; for the nails of His cross crucified me with Him. And now the essence of this new life is no longer mine, for the Anointed One lives His life through me—we live in union as one!

My new life is empowered by the faith of the Son of God who loves me so much that He gave Himself for me and dispenses His life into mine. My faith in Jesus transfers God's righteousness to me, and He now declares me flawless in His eyes.

I now enjoy true and lasting peace with all because of what Jesus has done for me. My faith guarantees me permanent access into this marvelous kindness that has given me a perfect relationship with You. What incredible joy bursts forth within me as I keep on celebrating my hope of experiencing Your glory!

That's not all! Even in times of trouble, I have a joyful confidence, knowing that these pressures will develop in me patient endurance. And patient endurance will refine my character, and proven character leads me back to hope. This hope is not a disappointing fantasy because I can now experience Your endless love cascading into my heart through the Holy Spirit who lives in me!

SCRIPTURE REFERENCES

Galatians 2:20 TPT • Ephesians 5:1-5 TPT

Faith Turns Hope into Reality

FATHER, thank You for the faith that brings my hopes into reality and becomes the foundation I need to acquire the things I long for. Faith empowers me to see that the universe was created and beautifully coordinated by the power of Your words! You spoke, and the invisible realm gave birth to all that is seen.

By constantly using my faith, the life of Christ will be released deep inside me, and the resting place of Your love will become the very source and root of my life. Then I will be empowered to discover what every holy one experiences—the great magnitude of the astonishing love of Christ in all its dimensions.

How deeply intimate and far reaching is Your love—enduring and inclusive! Endless love beyond measurement transcends my understanding. This extravagant love pours into me until I am filled to overflowing with the fullness of You, my Father. I will never doubt Your mighty power that works in me to accomplish all this. You will achieve infinitely more than my greatest request, my most unbelievable dream, and exceed my wildest imagination.

Father, You will outdo them all, for Your miraculous power constantly energizes me. God, I offer up to You all the glorious praise that rises from every church in every generation through Jesus Christ—and all that will yet be manifest through time and eternity. Amen.

SCRIPTURE REFERENCES

Hebrews 11:1 TPT • Ephesians 3:17-21 TPT

Faith to Be the Real Me

FATHER-GOD, You made everything beautiful and appropriate in its time. You have also planted eternity, a sense of divine purpose, in my heart—a mysterious longing which nothing under the sun can satisfy, except You!

Everything I could ever need for life and complete devotion to You has already been deposited in me by Your divine power. For all this was lavished upon me through the rich experience of knowing You!

You call me by name and invite me to come to You through a glorious manifestation of Your goodness. You have given me Your magnificent promises that are beyond all price, so through the power of these tremendous promises, I can experience partnership with the divine nature by which I have escaped the corrupt desires that are in the world!

Thank You, my Father. In Jesus' name I pray, amen.

SCRIPTURE REFERENCES

Ecclesiastes 3:11 AMPC • 2 Peter 1:3-4 TPT

Learning to Love

FATHER, thank You for the Holy Spirit who has imparted Your love until it overflows into my heart. I ask You to remove the streaks of selfishness that trip me up sometimes. I love You because You first loved me, and this is a love that never stops loving. It's greater than the gift of prophecy, which eventually will fade away. It is more enduring than tongues, which will one day fall silent. This love will remain long after words of knowledge are forgotten.

When I was a child, I spoke about childish matters, for I saw things like a child and reasoned like a child. But by the grace of God, the day came when I longed to mature and set aside my childish ways. Though I see but a faint reflection of riddles and mysteries, as though reflected in a mirror, I know that one day I will see face-to-face. My understanding may be incomplete now, but one day I will understand everything, just as everything about me has been fully understood.

Until then, I cherish the three things that remain: faith, hope, and love. Above all else, I choose to let love be the beautiful prize for which I run. It's all in the name of Jesus.

SCRIPTURE REFERENCES

Romans 5:1-5 • 1 Corinthians 13 TPT

God's Garden Under Cultivation

FATHER, thank You for choosing me to be Your garden under cultivation. My inward life is now sprouting, bringing forth fruit. What a beautiful paradise that unfolds within me. Your life is flowing into mine, pure as a garden spring; a well of living water springs up from within me, like a mountain brook flowing into my heart!

May Your awakening breath blow upon my life until I am fully yours. Breathe upon me with your Spirit wind; stir up the sweet spice of Your life within me. Spare nothing as You make me Your fruitful garden. Hold nothing back until I release Your fragrance. Thank You for pouring out refreshing water when I am thirsty.

I trust You to pour out of Your Spirit on my children, Your blessings upon my descendants. You are my Guide, and You will show me where to go and what to do. You will fill me with refreshment even when I am in a dry place. You continually restore strength to me so I will flourish like a well-watered garden and like an ever-flowing, trustworthy spring of blessing. In the name of Jesus, amen.

Scriptures References

1 Corinthians 3:9 AMPC • Song of Solomon 4:15 TPT
Isaiah 44:3 TPT • Isaiah 59:11 TPT

Believe You Are Who God Says You Are

LORD, You know everything there is to know about me, and You understand my every thought before it even enters my mind. I know that You are intimately aware of me, and You read my heart like an open book. You knew me before you formed me in my mother's womb, and now You have called me to follow You. You are transforming me to walk the pathway of love. When You created me in the secret place, You placed eternity in my heart.

You are Love, and I am a partaker of Your divine nature. I am becoming the person You created me to be.

I believe that You are who You claim to be and that You are making me to be my true self, the child-of-God self. I am created in Your image, and I have the mind of Christ and hold the thoughts, feelings, and purposes of His heart.

Creator of heaven and earth, I am Your workmanship, created in Christ Jesus for good works, which you prepared beforehand that I should walk in them. I choose to see myself as a poem or a work of art, and I ask You to forgive me for disapproving the "self" You created me to be. I plan to live the good life—the more abundant life—that You planned for me, in the name of Jesus, amen.

SCRIPTURE REFERENCES

Psalm 139 TPT • Jeremiah 1:5 • John 1:12 MSG
1 Corinthians 2:16 AMPC • Matthew 4:18-19 • Ecclesiastes 3:11
Ephesians 2:10 AMPC, NKJV

The Best Is Yet to Come

DEAR Father, Your wisdom is something mysterious that goes deep into the interior of Your purposes. It's not lying around on the surface. It's not the latest message, but more like the oldest—what You determined as the way to bring out his best in us, long before we ever arrived on the scene.

The experts of our day haven't a clue about what this eternal plan is. If they had, they wouldn't have killed the Master of the God-designed life on a cross. That's why we have this scripture text: No one's ever seen or heard anything like this, never so much as imagined anything quite like it—what You have arranged for those who love You!

You have planned things never discovered or heard of before, things beyond our ability to imagine—these are the many things You have in store for all who love You.

Your Word says we should never doubt Your mighty power to work in us and accomplish all this. As I trust You, You will achieve infinitely more than my greatest request, my most unbelievable dream, and exceed my wildest imagination!

Glory to God in the church! Glory to God in Jesus! Glory down all the generations! Glory through all millennia! Oh, yes!

SCRIPTURE REFERENCES

1 Corinthians 2:9 Voice, TPT, MSG • Ephesians 3:20 Voice, MSG

Praise: Joy Unspeakable and Full of Glory

An old song echoes throughout the recesses of my being, and I'm filled with great expectations!

I have found His grace is all complete,
He supplieth every need;
While I sit and learn at Jesus' feet,
I am free, yes, free indeed.
I have found the pleasure I once craved,
It is joy and peace within;
What a wondrous blessing, I am saved
From the awful gulf of sin.
I have found that hope so bright and clear,
Living in the realm of grace;
Oh, the Savior's presence is so near,
I can see His smiling face.
I have found the joy no tongue can tell,
How its waves of glory roll;
It is like a great o'erflowing well,
Springing up within my soul.
Refrain:
It is joy unspeakable and full of glory,

Full of glory, full of glory;
It is joy unspeakable and full of glory,
Oh, the half has never yet been told.[47]

Lord, I'm bursting with joy over what You've done for me! My lips are full of perpetual praise. I'm boasting of You and all Your works, so let all who are discouraged take heart. Join me, everyone! Let's praise the Lord together. Let's make His name glorious to all. Listen to my testimony: I cried to God in my distress, and He answered me. He freed me from all my fears!

47 "Joy Unspeakable," Barney E. Warren, 1900, Public Domain

Testimony

Winning the Good Fight of Faith

By Lynn Copeland Sutton

AFTER 20 years and five kids, I found myself a single mom and another statistic of divorce. The holidays became a very difficult time for me personally, for several reasons. Some years at Christmas, I completely shut down—no tree, no decorations, no presents. I allowed my thoughts to control me. My thoughts would begin to walk me down a dark path, and for years, I willingly followed. This happened year after year for 10 years.

This year would be different. Circumstances in my life had not changed. In fact, in some ways, things were worse, but this year would be different as I chose to put into practice principles God had been teaching me the last 10 years. I decided that I would begin to take my thoughts captive. Isn't that what His Word told me to do? (2 Cor. 10:5). My thoughts were lies fed to me by the enemy of my soul for years—the enemy who wants to destroy me, my children, my calling, my peace, my joy, and my light.

As the thoughts of inadequacy began to bombard my mind, I began to stand and engage in the good fight. As one lie after another slipped into my thoughts, I started saying, at times out loud, "That's not true!" I began to mentally step back and think about what I was hearing and evaluate it with the truth of God's Word. Please understand, it wasn't an immediate turn around. I had to ask God to strengthen me, which He did. For the first time in years, I didn't get very far down the dark path before I turned around. Throughout the month of December, I would engage in a few more battles, but each one was a little shorter than the previous one.

As I sit and write these words today, the lies want to bombard my mind yet again, keeping me from sharing with you that there is freedom from depression. Your enemy will take every opportunity to hurl lies and insults at you with the intent to poison your thought life, leading you away from your Creator who knows you intimately and loves you unconditionally. Friends, the war was won on the cross, and victory is there for the taking! Take what is rightfully yours by beginning to address the lies disguised as your thoughts.

Lynn Copeland Sutton is Germaine Copeland's daughter and a member of the Prayers That Avail Much ministry board. She resides in Watkinsville, Georgia.

Testimony

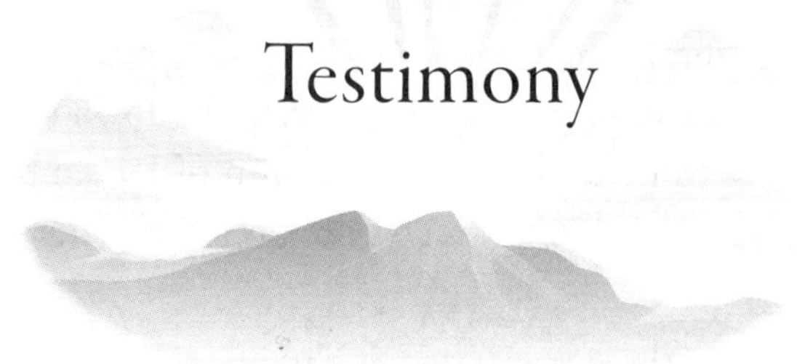

Don't Give Up! God Is on Your Side!

By Krissy Clark

My journey with depression has spanned most of my life. Although I am much better than I used to be, I feel like dealing with depression is an ongoing thing. Most days are better than others; however, there are many aspects of my life that the mere mention can drown me if I allow it.

One of my tricks is to give myself five to 10 minutes to go down the rabbit hole, but after that, I must give it to God. And usually, I remind myself numerous times that I have given it to Him. The biggest trick I have is that I try to forgive as quickly as I can. Colossians 3:13 tells us, "Bear with each other and forgive one another if any of you has a grievance against someone. Forgive as the Lord forgave you" (NIV).

I feel that one of the best ideas is finding a Christian counselor to talk to about your problems. I never felt any relief until I went to one who helped me break generational curses (Exodus 20:5), but most importantly, the counselor prayed with me and for me.

Above all, don't give up because God is on your side! Whatever you are going through, others have been through too, and they came out the other side healthy and happy. You know how everyone talks about the light at the end of the tunnel? That light is Jesus, and He is waiting for you. Just that thought has gotten me through some tough times, and it will get you through too!

Krissy Clark studied family advocacy and public policy at Liberty University. She received a Master of Arts in Human Services Counseling as well as a Bachelor of Arts in Psychology. Krissy resides in Athens, Georgia.

Germaine's Testimony

Testimony

BUT GOD! Depression Came to Destroy, But God Came to Deliver

By Germaine Copeland

SOMETHING strange was happening! The room where I was sitting disappeared, and I was standing at the edge of a brown, crusty field. In the far distance, I saw a farmer. The haunting, mocking sounds of death stopped as I stood there staring. The man walked to the far corner and plunged a sharp-pointed plow into the ground. Mesmerized, I watched as row after row was turned into beautiful, moist soil ready for planting. A dammed-up water supply burst, and I was crying a river.

The field was *me!*

Jesus Himself was the Farmer who appeared to me in a vision that cold January day to stop me from taking my own life.

Let me back up and tell you how I arrived at such a fateful day.

Depression was a dark, slimy pit where I lived for many years. In those days, there wasn't a name for it, but nevertheless, the agony was real. As the years wore on, ultimately, there was a day when suicide seemed the only way.

At times, I would turn over a new leaf and begin to find my way to peace. I even had an experience with God that was joy unspeakable and full of glory. But then, an older woman called to tell me that I could not expect to live on the mountain top, and another called to tell me I was going to hell because I had married outside our denomination. Again, thoughts bombarded my mind, and it wasn't long before depression returned with a vengeance. (Never forget—our words have power, and we must be sure that our "advice" to others lifts and gives hope!)

Depression was a dark, slimy pit where I lived for many years.

Like so many depressed people, I cried out, "Where is the God of the Bible? Why does He never answer me? Why are my silent screams met with silence? 'They' say that I'm this way because I want to be, but **I do not want to be this way!** No one hears—no one believes me."

Depression and anxiety are no respecter of persons. They are horrific tormentors that can attach themselves to a little girl who has just experienced trauma or a teenager lacking in self-esteem or a grown man who thought he had it made with a successful marriage, business, and grandchildren. In much the same way, it attached itself to me.

In those early days of depression, my eyes were blinded, and I didn't know that I could choose life or death. I didn't know that I had a choice about anxiety and depression. I didn't know then that God would take my hand through the power of His Word and lift me out of the pit that robbed me of peace and a mind free and clear. During those years of agonizing depression and anxiety, I believed everyone would be happier without me.

A day came when I experienced a glorious deliverance from fear, anxiety, and depression. No one else was around. It was just me and God. In the moment, in the twinkling of an eye, my darkness turned to light!

The Divine Helper

Deliverance is always supernatural, and everyone's experience is different. Yet, every deliverance is the beginning of an exciting faith adventure. God has prepared the way we are to walk, and we each have our personal journey with Him. In His kindness, He follows behind us to spare us from the harm of our past, and each past is different.[48]

Depression and anxiety are mental health issues that are sometimes passed down from generation to generation. Today, there is even medical and psychological help, and we have tools for achieving mental health. "A growing body of evidence shows how our thought lives have incredible power over our intellectual, emotional, cognitive, and physical well-being."[49]

Nevertheless, the lasting Cure is God. He has given you His Word and a Divine Helper who hovers over you. He has provided everything you need to walk in victory! In fact, He is your divine Helper! "For although we live in the natural realm [where mental disorders dwell], we don't wage a military campaign employing human weapons, *using manipulation to achieve our aims*. Instead, our *spiritual* weapons are energized with divine power to effectively dismantle the defenses *behind which people hide*. We can demolish every deceptive fantasy that opposes God and break through every arrogant attitude that is raised up in defiance of the true knowledge of God. We capture, like prisoners of war, every thought and insist that it bow in obedience to the Anointed One. *Since we are armed with such dynamic weaponry*, we stand ready to punish any trace of rebellion, as soon as you choose complete obedience."[50]

Scripture teaches us that thoughts are powerful! For as a man *thinks* within himself, so is he.[51] We no longer have to live in a fantasy world; we

48 Psalm 139 TPT

49 *Think, Learn and Succeed,* Dr. Caroline Leaf, pg. 34

50 2 Corinthians 10:3-6 TPT

51 Proverbs 23:7

can live in the reality of righteousness, peace, and joy—the reality of the way of love! We have the power to change the way we think! And this book from cover to cover is full of His counsel! As we align our lives with the truths therein, we'll find ourselves living in the peace and abundant life our Father promises. My life is a testimony to the power of God's Word.

The Counterattack

Many years after God delivered me from depression, it dared to raise its ugly head once again in an altogether different way. By that time, I was established as a Bible teacher and a writer whose books were changing the lives of people around the world. I traveled and ministered to crowds, sharing about prayer, faith, and walking in all the promises of God's Word. I was the pastor of a congregation I loved. Yet, as we've said, none of us is immune to depression—nor its counterattacks.

Anxiety was just a word to me until the afternoon of a similar experience a few weeks earlier. I pulled into the same parking lot, where I sat in my car staring across the street for a few minutes before opening the door to exit. Suddenly, the same sensation came over me, and another explosion happened. For the first time, I acknowledged that I was face to face with anxiety.

Could this be a panic attack? I wondered. Some would say, "Yes!" The loving Voice I had come to recognize spoke, "You need emotional healing. You have forgotten a past that has not forgotten you."

For the first and only time in my life, I put out a fleece before God. I said, "God, if this is really You, You will have to bring a counselor to me. I am not going to look for one!" God is faithful, and the day came when I attended a behavior modification class, which the diet center near my home was sponsoring. Wouldn't you know the speaker was a counselor, and I recognized his information was simply biblical principles. I spoke to him after the meeting and made an appointment with him. I expected to go in for a couple of sessions.

Over the period of a few years, buried feelings and unacknowledged anger and their origins were uncovered and resolved. Ed Lauria challenged everything I believed! The Wonderful Counselor, the Holy Spirit, speaks through men and women. God intended for us to be a community where we are helpers of each other's joy and share each other's burdens. Instead of hiding our true selves from one another, we overcome the fear of exposure and confess to one another our faults (our slips, our false steps, our offenses, our sins) and pray also for one another, that we may be healed and restored to a spiritual tone of mind and heart. The earnest (heartfelt, continued) prayer of a righteous man makes tremendous power available dynamic in its working.[52]

My healing came through fellowship with other like-minded believers, by being honest with myself and with them. I attended a codependency support group where I learned how to submit to the planting of the Lord. Remember, I am His field under cultivation.

These events only increased my faith in the One who "understands humanity." God knew the intimate details of the anxiety attacks. He knew me. And, again, intimate fellowship with my Father-God and His Word led me out to the calm and peaceful life He promises us. You and I are invited to come freely and boldly to where love is enthroned, receive mercy's kiss, and discover the grace we urgently need to strengthen us in our time of depression and anxiety.[53] Jesus promised if we would come unto Him, we would find rest for our souls.

52 James 5:16 AMPC

53 Hebrews 4:14-15 TPT

The Story of How My Depression Began

When did those two huge, ugly black birds named Depression and Anxiety first begin sitting outside my window? A very long time ago. It really began when my younger sister died at age 10 months.

While the two of us were playing together, I watched her die in a freakish accident.

While the two of us were playing together, I watched her die in a freakish accident. My dad came and grabbed her while others swooped in and whisked me away. That tragic circumstance altered my life. I was no longer a carefree, happy two-and-a-half-year-old child who loved to play. For years when my mother and dad began talking about Frieda, an adult would hurry me out of the room. It would be years before I asked my parents why they never allowed me to grieve with them. I was there, and I saw her die! Because of my age, everyone believed I was too young to understand. Little did they know that I would blame myself for her death.

Before you judge my parents and the adults who came to help them, remember when Jesus opened a man's blind eyes. Someone asked Jesus whose sin caused this guy's blindness, his own or the sin of his parents? Jesus answers, "Neither. It happened to him so that you could watch him experience God's miracle."[54] So no one caused the dark cloud of depression that followed me for many years.

The "stronghold of depression" began as a work of the flesh. I describe depression as a wall of defense to situations that hurt us. I remember once telling my mother that "I lived behind my eyelids," which was my childlike way of explaining I lived in a world to myself—quiet and self-isolated from the emotional fray. When a child is left to his or her own

54 John 9:1-5

thoughts, the child finds a way to survive the trauma. Within those walls we create a fantasy world where we can shut out the people around us. I escaped into a world of books and music.

Looking back, it's such childish thinking, but I thought that God had intended to take me instead of her and that He made a mistake. This was the lie that eventually opened the door to thoughts of ending my life years later.

Looking back, it's such childish thinking, but I thought that God had intended to take me instead of her and that He made a mistake.

No one could have foreseen the tragedy that claimed my sister's life, and I did not know how to process it. I was a child, and I thought like a child. If only someone would have spoken a good word to me maybe it would have been different, but that's not what happened. People held me and loved me, but no one acknowledged my broken heart. As adults, they did the best they knew to do with a child less than three years old.

I still vividly remember thinking the day of the accident that if I had died instead of my sister, my parents would be happy. Even though I was so young, I tried to make them happy, but in my childish mind, I failed.

Again and again, I attempted to prove I was good enough by climbing never-ending ladders of perfectionism. I climbed and climbed until the thought that God had made a mistake became my reality. Another lie was added to reinforce a lie that I had forgotten. That original thought became a mindset, which led me to believe that I should never have been born.

Moving forward many years, after marriage and the birth of our fourth child, the thought that I was harmful to my four children hounded my every step. A war raged inside me, and I wondered if I was mentally ill. I felt like two people at times. Standing at my stove, I looked up to see an image staring at me through the window. A haunting and sarcastic voice said, "There is a name for this. You are schizophrenic!" Little did I understand that war, which is described in Galatians the fifth chapter. I had been born again at the age of twelve, and the raging war inside was between my carnal mind and my spirit. The Spirit of Truth makes us free, and the war between the carnal mind and the mind controlled by the Spirit is real. One leads to death, the other to life and peace.[55]

My dad was a pastor, and we moved often. I looked forward to the move because I thought each location would change things for me or make life better. I experienced hope, which soon was lost in the shadow that was my constant companion. With each move, I was the new kid on the block, and initially, everyone acted like they wanted to be my friend. So, I learned to wait for people to approach me. But in small town U.S.A., the outsider remains the outsider. I tried, but I never fit in. People accused me of being snobbish and conceited. They had no idea I was just trying to survive. What did it matter anyway? I knew there would be another town, another church, another school, and other people.

Once again, I smiled while returning to my best friends—my books, my piano, and my studying. I really tried to be a "good example" for the church members' children. I was told that I could be anything I desired, but I soon learned that was not true. It was my responsibility to guard my dad's reputation. It didn't make sense to me, but the shadow that lived with me, that only I could see, made sure I saw how much fun the children in our church enjoyed life. But the more abundant life was only for certain people—it was all confusing.

God knew me before the foundation of the world, and He had placed a desire in me to study and know truth. I knew that I wanted to be a college English professor and a writer. I wanted to study psychology and

55 Romans 8:6

journalism. I had high hopes! I was denied college and told that I could teach piano without a degree. Teaching piano was not my goal in life. I blamed my dad until a day when I realized it was my own shadow I feared. I decided that God did not like me, and I did not like Him! My fear of going to hell where I would burn forever and a religious person who shared from the pulpit that all my nails would be pulled out with pliers if I did not serve God would not allow me to completely turn my back on God.

Depression is sneaky that way; it tricks us into becoming incredibly selfish until our feelings, our mistakes, our lack, our void, and our agony are all we can see.

Surely, everything would change when I started work, or so I thought. I loved my job, and they loved my work performance. With obvious regret, they fired me because I did not wear makeup, which the church told me was a sin. Satan takes advantage of every opportunity to build resentment that eventually leads to bitterness toward God. I made sure I was never fired from another job!

Of course, *if* I could just get married, *if* I could just have children, *if* I could go back to school and get my degree, it would all be better. I finally named my shadow of depression *If.* I married. I tried to be a PTA mom and fit in, but where was truth? All these other women both at school and in my neighborhood had it all together, and I wore many masks. *If* I had my degree, then I would be good enough to take my place in society.

With our three children in school, I was excited. Now I could go back to school. That was not to be. We make our plans, but God directs our steps.[56] Just as I was ready to enroll in school,

56 Proverbs 16:1

I discovered that I was to have another child. I fell in love with her the moment I held her in my arms. Who knew that in a few weeks I would be sitting with a bottle of pills ready to go to never-never land where I would sleep the sleep of the dead?

It is ludicrous now in reflection, but I believed that I was ending my life for the sake of my children. I look back and realize that it was lie upon lie upon lie that I believed. And who is the father of lies? Satan! It has been said that suicide is a permanent solution to a temporary feeling. Even though I had convinced myself that I was thinking of others, in reality, it was about me. Depression is sneaky that way; it tricks us into becoming incredibly selfish until our feelings, our mistakes, our lack, our void, and our agony are all we can see. Depression blinds us. It lies to us. Left to run its course, it points us toward death.

A Day of Reckoning

On January 20, 1968, the three older children were at school, and the baby was in her crib asleep. Sitting down with my cup of coffee, I felt secure in what I was about to do, looking for the exact time to take the bottle of sleeping pills. I was tired of trying to keep all the laws. What sense did it make to go to a movie and pray that Jesus wouldn't come back while I was in there?

I'll never forget the time my two brothers and my sister sat out in front of the house waiting for our parents to return home. I just knew that Jesus had come, and we were left because we were not good enough. I read all the self-help books. I knew all the Old Testament stories and tried to read the Bible. I tried to be good, but

Suddenly, I was no longer seated at my kitchen table that cold, dreary day in January with a bottle of pills in my hand ready to end it all.

My deliverance from the power of death came on the very day I had decided to end my life here on earth. Jesus had appeared to me, and my night was turned to day.

now I was faced with the fact that I was truly a mistake, living a lie and hurting my children. The hateful mocking voice spoke, "Why look at you! You are a weak person—even too weak to take a simple bottle of pills."

Whether aloud or from my heart I do not know, but with passion I cried, "God, if You are who my parents said You are, this is Your last chance to prove it! I refuse to go on this way! It's over. Do You hear me? It's over."

Jesus Plowed My Hardened Ground

Suddenly, I was no longer seated at my kitchen table that cold, dreary day in January with a bottle of pills in my hand ready to end it all. I was standing at the edge of a brown, cracked field of fallow ground. There was movement in the far right-hand corner, and I was mesmerized as a Farmer named Jesus struck the hardened ground with a sharp-pointed plow.

I couldn't move. I continued staring at the ground as beautiful, moist, fertile soil was turned up row by row. To my surprise, a dammed-up river of tears began cascading down my face. I was God's field under cultivation! Jesus had come to do the cultivating. He showed me the problem and the solution—and tended to the soil of my heart.

Suddenly, I was once again sitting at my kitchen table. I do not know how much time elapsed; it seemed like both seconds and an eternity. The table and everything around me was bathed in light. The walls were now a heavenly yellow. I looked outside to see brilliant evergreen trees welcoming me, and the overcast sky had turned into "blue skies smiling at me."

His loving Voice spoke to me and said, "Old things have passed away, and behold all things have become new!" Jesus had healed me heart and soul!

My deliverance from the power of death came on the very day I had decided to end my life here on earth. Jesus had appeared to me, and my night was turned to day.

Faith Not Feelings

That was a glorious day, but as I was to learn, we are destined to walk by faith and not by feelings. For three months, I was on cloud nine! I thought differently, I acted differently, and I saw differently. But slowly, depression began to edge its way back, diminishing the peace and joy I was beginning to know.

Then, as I sat on the front steps enjoying the sunshine one beautiful spring morning, the euphoric feelings disappeared. It seemed that fear sat on me and entangled me once again. I was afraid.

"God," I cried out, "If I have to go back to the way I was before, please take me now! I cannot live that way again!

The same tender-loving Voice that had spoken on the day of deliverance spoke once again, "My child, today is your first day of learning to walk by faith."

I arose and walked back into my kitchen where I sat every morning with my Bible, pen, and paper and became a student of God's Word.

I arose and walked back into my kitchen where I sat every morning with my Bible, pen, and paper and became a student of God's Word.

That was the beginning of an adventure that will someday return me to my eternal home beyond those evergreen trees and blue skies. In the meantime, I remain God's garden under cultivation.

God's Promise to You

You also are God's field under cultivation! Jesus already paid the price and uprooted fear, depression, anxiety, and other mental disorders.[57] He has planted you beside living waters where your leaf will not wither IF you continue in His Word. Keep praising the One who delivered you from darkness and translated you into the world of Light!

God is faithful to watch over His Word to perform it. I encourage you to choose Him and take His hand. He is the Truth, the Way, and the Life.

57 1 John 3:8; Hebrews 2:14 AMPC

A Message to Those Who Walk Beside Us

Admit your faults to one another and pray for each other so that you may be healed. The earnest prayer of a righteous man has great power and wonderful results.

James 5:16 TLB

Let Go and Let God

Meditation

It is not easy living with someone who suffers with any of the mental/emotional issues we address in this book. Maybe you are a parent who is desperate to find answers. You may experience guilt, anger, shame, and wonder where you missed it. After all, you love your child who is a gift from God.

Maybe you are the spouse of someone who is fearful, depressed, anxious, and angry. My husband, an engineer, has always believed if you have a problem, you fix it and move on. He is a faithful man who loved me during my most challenging times of anxiety and depression. After working all day, he came home to help with the children and the housework. He tried to talk to me, and today I know that he was telling me the truth. But at the time, my eyes were blinded. In his frustration, he withdrew emotionally.

This is not a parenting manual or a marriage manual. But this I know, there are answers and there is help! I found mine in the Secret Place with my Bible and the Holy Spirit. Be patient with yourself and with others. Remind yourself that each one is God's field under cultivation. Individually and together, you will be ever learning, ever growing, and ever achieving. It's a process!

Our homes are "mission" fields where we are to develop lasting relationships. It's not about religion. It's not about controlling another human being—not even our children. It's about making disciples. There are answers—we do not merely listen to the word, but we learn to live the Word by doing the Word.[58]

58 Matthew 7:24-26

Let's begin here and apply it to our homelives and those in our care.

My beloved friends, if you see a believer who is overtaken with a fault, may the one who overflows with the Spirit seek to restore him. Win him over with gentle words, *which will open his heart to you* and will keep you from exalting yourself over him. *Love empowers us* to fulfill the law of the Anointed One as we carry each other's troubles. If you think you are too important to stoop down to help another, you are living in deception (Galatians 6:1-3 TPT).

There is hope!

All the issues we address from cover to cover are a matter of family crisis. Those who want to help their loved ones need the wisdom of God to walk with them through the valleys, the rivers, the mud flats, the emotional ups and downs. There is a time to speak, a time to listen, and a time to remain quiet. There is an art to listening, and we can learn *how* to listen. There is also a time you must let go! Don't you love that infamous cliché? Let go and let God!

Just as we were, our children are born into a world of polarity. If only we could look at our homes as a "church" where we are teaching disciples who are here for God's purposes. First Corinthians 13 is something we read at weddings, but what would happen if we learned to walk this out in our homes? We must say to our children, "I'll always love you. I may not agree with your decisions, but always know that I love you!"

All our loved ones, including our children, have a road to walk, and we cannot walk that road for them no matter how much we try. They are God's handiwork, and He planned beforehand the paths that they should walk, which He prearranged and made ready for each of our children to live.[59]

Each situation is an opportunity to love the hurting person unconditionally with the "agape" love that has been shed abroad in our hearts by the Holy Spirit.[60]

59 Ephesians 2:10 AMPC

60 Romans 5:5

All the sections in this book up until now were written for the persons who have or are experiencing the various mental disorders. This meditation and this prayer are for you—the one who walks beside. In those days of darkest depression, my family never knew how I would be from one day to the next...sometimes from one moment to another. There did not seem to be a pattern—it is crazy and crazy-making!

In today's environment, there is help available! Thank God churches are now offering help.

There is no school of faith that equals the home. Your spouse is created in the image of God; your children are gifts from God. Unfortunately, too often we treat strangers with more respect than we do our family members. We receive emotional healing and grow spiritually in our relationships. This begins when two people come together in a healthy marriage to help and encourage each other to be the people God created them to be. In reality everything is about learning to walk the forgotten way—the way of love. It's really that simple. Simple does not indicate easy. Selfishness gets in the way. We are ALL growing spiritually and learning to walk in agape love, which begins with a decision. May we be lights shining in the darkness!

Jesus and the Holy Spirit are praying for you and the family member that you so desperately are trying to fix! Purpose to trust God with the outcome!

By the way...let go and let God! From someone who has been there, it may take time. It's all a process, but you will find there's no comparison between the present hard times and the coming good times.[61]

God is perfecting all that concerns you[62] and not one word of His good promises has ever failed to come to pass.[63]

---

61 Romans 8:18-21 MSG

62 Psalm 138:8

63 1 Kings 8:56

Prayer

Father, I know that I am to love my family with the love that springs from You. No matter how eloquently I speak, my words are reduced to the hollow sound of nothing more than a clanging cymbal if I do not love. Teach me to love ______________ as You have loved me.

My human love is subject to circumstances, but Your Love never fails. Lord, if love is not coming out of me and flowing toward even the most difficult member of my family, then I am in the greatest need myself. Your love is shed abroad in my heart by the Holy Spirit, and I live in the light. I choose not to cause ________ to stumble.

By faith I bind myself to Your will, purposes, truth, mind, mercy, grace, and love. I loose from myself the soulish irritation, frustration, resentment, anger, unforgiven offenses, and any unresolved issues I have hidden.[64] These difficult times expose that I sometimes reason like a child. Lord, I desire to mature and set aside my childish ways so I can speak grace-filled words. Teach me to love as You have loved me.

Thank You for imparting to me the riches of the Spirit of wisdom and the Spirit of revelation that I may know my Lord Jesus Christ through deepening intimacy with Him. Thank You that the eyes of my understanding are flooded with light and illuminated. Thank You for the immeasurable greatness of Your power made available to me through faith. My life will be an advertisement of this immense power as it works through me. The light of Your truth floods in so that I benefit from all that You do know, not what I don't know. I grasp the immensity of this glorious way of life You have for Your followers. Oh, the utter extravagance of Your work in me—endless energy, boundless strength!

As I stick with Your Word, it sticks with me! Your powerful Word is sharp as a surgeon's scalpel, cutting through everything. That means no matter what I hear, Your Word will empower me to recognize truth.

64 *Breaking the Power*, Liberty Savard, pg. 188

Nothing and no one can resist God's Word. We can't get away from it—no matter what! Your Word cuts between soul and spirit, exposes innermost thoughts and desires, exposing and sifting and analyzing and judging the very thoughts and purposes of the heart.

I'm swift to hear, slow to speak, and slow to wrath. I harness my desire to speak, and I don't get worked up into a rage. In fact, the Holy Spirit helps me, and I never allow emotion to be the biggest thing in the room. I speak prompted by the Holy Spirit and speak wisdom that others cannot resist.

As I wait on You, You will renew my strength and power. I will run and not be weary. I will walk and not faint or become tired. I will experience divine strength. I will run my race and helped my loved one run also without growing weary. I will walk through life without giving up!

SCRIPTURE REFERENCES

Romans 5:5 • James 1:1 • 1 Corinthians 13 • 1 John 2:10 TPT
Ephesians 1:17-19 TPT, MSG, Voice • Hebrews 4:12 MSG, AMPC
James 1:19 MSG, Voice • Acts 6:10 TPT • Isaiah 40:31 AMPC, TPT

Resources

Think, Learn, Succeed: Understanding and Using Your Mind to Thrive at School, the Workplace, and Life — Dr. Caroline Leaf

The Perfect You: A Blueprint for Identity — Dr. Caroline Leaf

The Combat Trauma Healing Manual: Christ-centered Solutions for Combat Trauma — Chris Adsit

The Way of Love — Ted Dekker

Shattering Your Strongholds: Freedom from Your Struggles — Liberty Savard

The Road Less Traveled — M. Scott Peck, M.D.

Choice Theory: A New Psychology of Personal Freedom — William Glasser, M.D.

Facing Codependence: What It Is, Where It Comes From, How It Sabotages Our Lives — Pia Mellody with Andrea Wells Miller and J. Keith Miller

Prayers That Avail Much for Your Family — Germaine Copeland

"Bible Verses for Overcoming Grief" — Bible Study Tools: https://www.biblestudytools.com/topical-verses/bible-verses-for-overcoming-grief/

About the Author

GERMAINE Copeland is the author of the bestselling *Prayers That Avail Much*® book series. Founder and president of Word Ministries, Inc., Germaine has traveled nationally and internationally, conducting prayer schools and speaking at churches and conferences.

Today, her ministry reaches around the world through her books and teaching videos. Germaine and her husband, Everette, have four children, eleven grandchildren, and a growing number of great-grandchildren and great-great grandchildren.

Mission Statement

Word Ministries, Inc.

To motivate individuals to spiritual growth and emotional wholeness, encouraging them to become more deeply and intimately acquainted with Father-God as they pray prayers that avail much.

Contact Word Ministries by writing:

Word Ministries, Inc.

P. O. Box 289

Good Hope, GA 30641

(770) 267-7603

www.prayers.org

Please include your testimonies
and praise reports when you write!

Other Bestselling Books in the *Prayers That Avail Much*® series

Prayers That Avail Much® 40th Anniversary Edition

Prayers That Avail Much® Gold-Letter Gift Edition

Prayers That Avail Much® Volume 1

A Global Call to Prayer

Prayers That Avail Much® for New Believers

Prayers That Avail Much® for Your Family

Prayers That Avail Much® for Women – pocket edition

Prayers That Avail Much® for Men – pocket edition

Prayers That Avail Much® for Parents

Prayers That Avail Much® for Moms – pocket edition

Prayers That Avail Much® for Mothers

Prayers That Avail Much® for Grandparents

Prayers That Avail Much® for Young Adults

Prayers That Avail Much® for the College Years

Prayers That Avail Much® for Teens

Prayers That Avail Much® for the Workplace

Prayers That Avail Much® for Leaders

Prayers That Avail Much® 365-Day Devotional

365 Days to a Prayer-Filled Life

Prayers That Avail Much® for America

Prayers That Avail Much® for the Nations

Prayers That Avail Much® for Graduates

OUR VISION

Proclaiming the truth and the power of the Gospel of Jesus Christ with excellence. Challenging Christians to live victoriously, grow spiritually, know God intimately.